EXITING
IRAQ

EXITING IRAQ: WHY THE U.S. MUST END THE MILITARY OCCUPATION AND RENEW THE WAR AGAINST AL QAEDA

REPORT OF A SPECIAL TASK FORCE
CHRISTOPHER PREBLE, DIRECTOR

CATO INSTITUTE
Washington, D.C.

Library of Congress Cataloging-in-Publication Data

Exiting Iraq : why the U.S. must end the military occupation and
    renew the war against Al Qaeda : a Cato Institute special task
    force report / Christopher Preble, director.
        p. cm.
    ISBN 1-930865-64-3
        1. Iraq War, 2003. 2. War on Terrorism, 2001– 3.   Qaida
    (Organization)   I. Preble, Christopher A.   II. Cato Institute.
    III. Title.

    DS79.76.E95 2004
    956.7044'31—dc22

                                                              2004051876

Cover design by Elise Rivera.
Cover photo credit: Copyright 2004, USA TODAY. Reprinted with
permission.
Printed in the United States of America.

                        CATO INSTITUTE
            1000 Massachusetts Ave., N.W.
                  Washington, D.C. 20001

Contents

Foreword

Speculation on the prospects for success or failure, loosely defined, in postwar Iraq has become a growth industry. Many reports and studies were published in the months before the United States launched military operations to remove Saddam Hussein from power. Dozens more have been published in the months since Hussein's regime collapsed. Although the recommendations of those reports are as varied as the many authors who wrote them, nearly all emphasize the need to achieve political and economic stability in Iraq. Most recommend a long-term U.S. or international commitment to the country, or both. Many call on the United States to establish a democratic system of government there. A few place additional conditions on judging the ultimate success, or failure, of America's Iraqi intervention, from the guarantee of basic human rights for women and ethnic or religious minorities; to the provision of health care services to all Iraqis; to the mandate that all Iraqi children, girls as well as boys, be afforded educational opportunities.

Such recommendations are based on the presumption that the achievement of such goals in Iraq is essential to American interests—that they are, indeed, intrinsic American interests. The well-being of Iraqis, their access to education, and their legal status are presumed to be nearly synonymous with the safety and well-being of American citizens.

Much of this discussion, while well-intentioned, distracts us from what should be America's core policy objectives. The overwhelming focus on the fate of Saddam; on how to contain the Iraqi insurgency; on how to reconcile the competing aspirations of Shias, Sunnis, and Kurds within a democracy; and on how to provide power, water, and other basic services has relegated to the background a much more fundamental question: what are America's national security interests in Iraq?

In December 2003, I convened a task force of scholars and policy experts to examine the core question of U.S. strategic interests in

Iraq. Our unequivocal finding, that it is in America's interest to quickly end the military occupation of Iraq, is so at variance with the conventional wisdom that it suggests that we adhere to a far different set of assumptions than those that have seemed to guide Washington's pre- and postwar policy up to this point. The Bush administration argues, "We must stay as long as necessary." Many people quibble over what is "necessary," but most implicitly endorse an open-ended commitment. In contrast, the authors of this report are unified in their opposition to the presumption that "we must stay."

This report was written before the scheduled handover of sovereignty from the Coalition Provisional Authority headed by Amb. L. Paul Bremer to a new Iraqi government. The handover occurred two days before the original deadline of June 30, 2004, but much remains to be done. It is in America's best interest to withdraw its military from Iraq at the earliest possible date, and the transfer of political sovereignty is the first crucial step in that process.

But to focus too much attention on the political transition is to ignore the far larger problem for Americans and the far greater long-term threat to American interests: the U.S. military occupation of Iraq. Regardless of when the handover of sovereignty actually takes place, the U.S. military intends to be in Iraq long afterwards. It is this aspect of the Bush administration's plans that warrants special attention, because a long-term military presence in Iraq undermines the very goals that we are hoping to achieve there: it emboldens anti-American terrorists to expand their operations, both against the forces in their neighborhood and ultimately on American soil. And the presence of an American military garrison in Iraq weakens the forces of democratic reform by undermining an indigenous government's authority and credibility. Accordingly, this report contains recommendations for a dramatic shift in policy away from U.S. military occupation and toward a sovereign and independent Iraq responsible for, and capable of, defending itself.

I want to thank the members of the task force for their work on this important project. They all made time in their busy schedules to contribute. On a personal note, I must recognize Jerod Partin, a research intern at the Cato Institute, for all of the work that he has done on this project. As a former intern myself, I have great respect for all of the great work that interns do. Jerod's efforts, however, have gone well above and beyond the call of duty, and he deserves special thanks and praise. Additional thanks go to the editorial staff and to those responsible for publishing and promoting this important study, and for the financial and institutional support provided by the Cato Institute.

Christopher Preble
Director
Exiting Iraq Task Force

Executive Summary

The United States must promptly end its military occupation of Iraq. A military withdrawal will maximize America's ability to refocus its efforts on the fight against Al Qaeda and other anti-American terrorist groups with global reach and, at the same time, minimize the risks to vital U.S. national security interests.

The occupation is counterproductive in the fight against radical Islamic terrorists and actually increases support for Osama bin Laden in Muslim communities not previously disposed to support his radical interpretation of Islam. Given the failure to find weapons of mass destruction (WMD) in Iraq, and the similar failure to establish a linkage between Saddam Hussein and Al Qaeda, the military occupation of Iraq can be made to look like the second phase of a U.S. war of conquest by individuals such as bin Laden who hunger for a civilizational clash between Muslims and non-Muslims.

The U.S. troop presence in Iraq is burdensome, in terms of both lives lost and dollars spent, and completely unnecessary. The dollar costs are likely to exceed $50 billion per year. Rather than spend such vast sums over and above the $400 billion spent annually for defense, the United States should use the advantages that its military spending has purchased. The United States is capable of fighting Al Qaeda in a variety of ways, few, if any, of which require military invasion and occupation of enemy states. Even in those rare instances in which the use of overwhelming military force is warranted, such operations rarely require the stationing of U.S. troops in foreign lands. The recent war in Iraq and the previous operation in Afghanistan demonstrate the American military's enormous capability for power projection over great distances.

A calculation of the true costs of the military occupation of Iraq must also include the strains imposed on the U.S. military. Absent a firm commitment to quickly reduce, and then eliminate, the military presence in Iraq, more and more will be demanded of the men and women in uniform. Those burdens threaten to undermine the

1

recruitment and retention that are key to the health of the all-volunteer force.

Given that the military mission is not essential to protecting U.S. security, the occupation of Iraq poses unnecessary risks to U.S. soldiers and Marines. Our soldiers are already subjected to daily attacks from all sides. The attacks extend to innocent Iraqis who are attempting to take control of their own lives but are ostracized and targeted as collaborators by their fellow Iraqis. The end of the foreign occupation will seriously undermine the terrorists' claims that their acts of violence against Iraqis are somehow serving the interests of Iraq.

As dangerous as the current situation in Iraq is for our troops and for average Iraqis, the risks extend much further. If our forces remain in Iraq indefinitely, they may well find themselves caught in the middle of a civil war between Iraq's feuding ethnic and religious factions. Some observers have justified a long-term U.S. presence on the grounds that our troops will prevent such a conflict from occurring. On the contrary, those forces may succeed in temporarily stifling ethnic tensions, but true reconciliation can come only from Iraqis themselves and will likely take many years. Meanwhile, the U.S. forces are a lightning rod for domestic dissent and rebellion, paving the way for intervention by Iraq's neighbors coming to the aid of coreligionists across the border in the event of full-scale armed conflict.

The prospects for creating liberal democracy in Iraq are bleak; the ambitious goal of creating even a stable *illiberal* government certainly cannot be achieved in the near term. Whatever government emerges from the chaos and violence must command the respect of Iraq's disparate religious and ethnic groups. It must possess legitimacy in the eyes of the Iraqi people. It will be difficult if not impossible for a fledgling government to prove that it is serving the popular will if it is seen as dependent on the U.S. military for its survival.

In the highly unlikely event that an American military occupation aided the installation of a democratic government in Iraq, such a government would not necessarily support American interests. Given the virulent anti-American sentiments in the country and throughout the Middle East, an Iraqi government that represented the wishes of the people could well choose to support Al Qaeda or other anti-American terrorist groups that seek our destruction. Accordingly, U.S. policies should not be predicated on the installation of a liberal democratic government in Iraq; U.S. policymakers should focus instead on the policies adopted by the government that emerges.

The withdrawal of U.S. forces must be coupled with a clear and unequivocal message to the people of Iraq: do not threaten us; do not support anti-American terrorists; do not develop weapons of mass destruction. If you do, we will be back.

That message must be communicated publicly because it is a message that must be understood throughout the international community. Other countries have nothing to fear from the United States if they disavow support for terrorist groups that aim to kill American citizens. But as the Taliban learned, America's ability to eliminate direct threats to U.S. security does not depend on a permanent military garrison in a foreign land.

In the interest of strengthening the interim Iraqi government and of expediting the military withdrawal, the United States should encourage the widest possible representation of Iraq's religious and ethnic minorities and should not demand that the new government be organized around a strong central authority based in Baghdad. If Iraq's disparate ethnic communities opt for some measure of autonomy, the United States should not stand in the way of a federal solution. However, Iraqis must understand that they will be responsible for defending themselves from both internal and external threats.

Negotiations over the U.S. military withdrawal should be initiated with the new interim government immediately after the handover of sovereignty, and all U.S. troops should be withdrawn by the time of nationwide elections, stipulated in the interim constitution to take place not later than January 31, 2005.

Introduction

A prompt end to the U.S. military occupation of Iraq is the sole acceptable solution to a vexing problem that threatens to seriously harm U.S. interests. The U.S. occupation of Iraq has already cost the lives of hundreds of American servicemen and servicewomen. A few thousand more have been wounded, many of them grievously. Casualty figures for Iraqi civilians are even higher. The Associated Press reported that at least 3,240 Iraqi civilians were killed during the combat phase of operations (from March 19 to May 1, 2003), and estimates of the numbers killed and wounded since then vary widely. A review of morgue records concluded that more than 5,500 Iraquis died violently in the first 12 months of the occupation.[1] The occupation is costing, on average, more than $4 billion per month, and there are no plans to reduce the number of forces in the country. Many voices, on both the left and the right, have called for a dramatic increase in the number of men and women deployed in Iraq and have also called for an explicit pledge that those forces will remain in the country for an extended period of time. The costs of the occupation of Iraq, therefore, in both lives and dollars, can only increase.

The military occupation of Iraq is not merely costly and burdensome for the United States; it is also counterproductive in the fight against anti-American terrorists. The first effects can be seen in the diplomatic harm that has come to the United States in a host of settings, as few countries have been willing to support U.S. actions in Iraq. International cooperation is essential to eliminating the sources of financial support for transnational terrorists and is equally crucial to ensuring that terrorists operating in foreign lands are captured, prosecuted, convicted, and punished. In recent months, a number of suspected terrorists have been set free in countries where the people do not share Americans' perspectives on the nature of the terrorist threat.[2]

Those ruptures can be repaired. The process of reconciliation should begin with a forthright admission that American goals in

Iraq were overly, even recklessly, ambitious. U.S. policymakers can admit that the warnings of our erstwhile allies about the likely conditions in postwar Iraq have proved sadly prescient. Although the United States may suffer a short-term loss of prestige after a military withdrawal, it is unlikely that any other nation-state will interpret that diplomatic setback as a reflection of the U.S. government's inability to defend the security and safety of Americans.

State actors do not pose the greatest threat to U.S. vital security interests; the far greater threat to the lives and well-being of average Americans comes from the transnational terrorists who operate in dozens of countries around the globe and who refuse to abide by the accepted norms of international behavior. Although the U.S. withdrawal from Iraq might be celebrated as a short-term victory for the jihadis, the end of the U.S. military occupation would actually weaken those terrorists over the long term because Al Qaeda and other anti-American terrorist groups have used the U.S. occupation as a vehicle for promulgating their message of hatred and violence. By ending the humiliating U.S. military presence in Iraq, the United States will deprive those murderers of one of their most reliable recruiting tools. Meanwhile, bringing an end to the occupation also allows the United States to refocus its military and intelligence assets on the fight against terrorists who seek to murder Americans.

America's ability to fight Al Qaeda is not contingent upon the emergence of liberal democracy in Iraq; we therefore reject the contention that the creation of a democratic Iraq should be a central goal of U.S. policy. Even if it were possible to create such a government at gunpoint, we do not presume that U.S. interests will automatically be protected under an Iraqi government committed to democratic principles. By the same token, we do not presume that a government *not* committed to those principles would be automatically hostile to the United States. Simply put, a government chosen by popular vote might sympathize with Osama bin Laden; one maintained by force might seek his destruction.

A democratic, prosperous, and free Iraq would of course be preferable to an Iraq ruled by tyrants. To focus solely on the installation of a democratic government, and not on the policies adopted by that government once it is in place, however, would be a grave error. Given that anti-American sentiments are rampant throughout the

Middle East, democratic elections could produce governments hostile to the United States, particularly if the particular democracy instituted is seen as having been dictated at American gunpoint.

Therefore, a U.S. military withdrawal should not be predicated on the establishment of a democratic government in Iraq. There is a clear distinction between core U.S. national interests (in other words, those interests worth fighting for) and goals that, while they may be worthy, are not, and should not be, the central object of U.S. foreign policy. We welcome the emergence of a new government in Iraq. We believe that a liberal democratic government can eventually develop and that its development can be stimulated by trade and economic interaction. We welcome the participation of private groups and nongovernmental organizations in supporting institutions of civil society that promote political and economic freedom. But we doubt that those goals can or should be advanced through the use of military power, specifically a long-term U.S. military presence in Iraq.

Observers who criticize plans for a relatively swift handover of sovereignty to an Iraqi government, and who expect the U.S. military to remain in Iraq for many years, assume that the United States has the moral authority, the wisdom, and the wherewithal to craft a perfect solution for Iraq.

We don't. The United States must end the military occupation of Iraq because, regardless of what we do, our effort to remake Iraq in our image will fail. U.S. policy should be directed toward an acceptable, if imperfect, end: one that minimizes the risks to U.S. vital security interests while maximizing our opportunities to refocus our efforts on the fight against Al Qaeda and other anti-American terrorist groups with global reach. Finally, by advocating an acceptable and achievable option focused on U.S. vital security interests, we do not presume that the United States will lose all interest in Iraqi affairs.

There is a host of possible outcomes in post-Hussein Iraq; many of them are unpalatable from a humanitarian perspective, but very few of them pose a direct threat to American security interests. For example, it is possible that a Baathist-style secular government will emerge, dedicated to holding Iraq's fractious polity together by suppressing religious and ethnic identities in favor of Arab nationalism. That was the approach adopted by Saddam Hussein, and it was also favored by British authorities responsible for suppressing Iraqis in the early to mid 20th century.

A more likely scenario, given the widespread rejection of secularism as a governing principle for Iraq, is the emergence of radical Islam as a viable political movement, with state structures guided by Islamic law. Such a state can be expected to suppress the rights of women and non-Muslims and might even preach violence against nonbelievers. A third possibility is the disintegration of Iraq into three or more states organized along ethno-religious lines. Under each of those scenarios, Iraqi leaders could willingly ignore foreigners' recommendations about how the Iraqi internal political system should operate and at the same time agree not to threaten American citizens and our vital interests.

The United States must remain committed to the enforcement of certain norms. The new government in Iraq, regardless of its precise composition or character, must understand in no uncertain terms that the United States will insist on certain behavior: do not threaten us; do not support anti-American terrorists; do not develop weapons of mass destruction.

Because the U.S. military and U.S. taxpayers did for the Iraqi people what they would not, or could not, do for themselves—namely rid their country of a murderous, tyrannical dictator—it is not unreasonable that we would be interested in developments in Iraq for the foreseeable future. But that does not mean that the United States must station troops in Iraq or elsewhere in the Middle East.

The same approach applies in both Iraq and Afghanistan and can be boiled down as follows: "We're out, and we are not responsible for your security. But we'll be watching you." That might mean an agreement with the Iraqi government on mechanisms for monitoring its conduct for several years. It could include U.S. liaison officers or a special diplomatic mission attached to the Iraqi defense ministry. And, since fighting against Al Qaeda and other anti-American terrorist groups is and should be a core object of U.S. policy, the United States should be willing to provide the new government with some assistance in the military and intelligence realms specific to fighting terrorism.

The other policy recommendations contained in this report are based on the presumption that American national security policy should seek to preserve American security, not remake other societies. The authors further presume that the leading threat to American security is Al Qaeda and its affiliated terrorist organizations that have demonstrated the capability and the intent to cause harm to American citizens and American interests, both here in the United States and abroad. The sole guiding criterion, therefore, for judging the success or failure of American policy in postwar Iraq is the relationship between the new government in Iraq and the anti-American terrorist organizations dedicated to our destruction. If the new government in Iraq welcomes Al Qaeda into its country, if the new government provides material support to Al Qaeda cells both in Iraq and abroad, if the new government seeks to obtain WMD, then our policies in Iraq will have failed. By contrast, if the new government of Iraq prevents Al Qaeda from operating within its borders; if the new government cooperates with U.S. intelligence and law enforcement agencies in identifying, tracking, and, where possible, eliminating Al Qaeda; if it pledges to develop and maintain military forces solely for the purpose of defending itself from threats, then our policy with respect to post-Saddam Iraq will have been a success.

American efforts in Iraq should be limited, focusing on the swift transition to an Iraqi interim government empowered to move toward full self-government. Beyond that, the United States must be willing to accept the wishes of the Iraqi people and should not assume that a friendly government can or should be imposed at the barrel of a gun. It may be unfair to characterize the new government in Iraq as an American puppet—but such sentiments are sure to persist, no matter what the United States does to insulate the government from such charges, if Washington insists on a prolonged military presence in the country. It will be far more difficult to prove the new government's legitimacy and credibility if it is seen as dependent on the U.S. military for its survival.

The United States need not have troops in Iraq to ensure that the country does not threaten American interests. Drawing on its economic assets and its political standing, the United States will continue to exert enormous influence in the region. In the event that regional conditions directly threaten vital U.S. security interests, the United States can call upon the U.S. military's capacity for projecting force over great distances to counter those threats.

A long-term American troop presence in Iraq is not merely unnecessary and counterproductive in terms of the fight against Al Qaeda and anti-American terrorists; it is also counterproductive in a wider sense, in terms of eroding America's standing around the world. Maintaining a permanent military presence in Iraq will be costly, both in dollars and in the hardships it imposes on the all-volunteer force. Such pressures are sure to weaken the United States, rendering us less capable of waging an effective fight against those individuals and groups who are the greatest threat to the United States. A draining and costly military occupation of Iraq will also undermine our ability to defend against more traditional threats to U.S. security from state actors.

For all those reasons, an expeditious military withdrawal from Iraq is in America's best interest. This report maps out that case and concludes with specific recommendations for conducting such a withdrawal.

1. A Long-Term Military Occupation of Iraq Is Not in the Best Interests of the United States

The American military's swift victory over the Baathist regime in Iraq in April 2003 set the stage for a shift in U.S. military deployments in the region. The shift began with Defense Secretary Donald Rumsfeld's announcement on April 29, 2003, less than three weeks after the fall of Baghdad, that U.S. troops would be removed from Saudi Arabia, where they had been stationed since late 1990. "It is now a safer region because of the change of regime in Iraq," the secretary said.[3] The withdrawal was implemented in short order, and all U.S. military personnel were out of the kingdom by the end of August.[4] Drawing on the early lessons learned from the just-concluded war, Rumsfeld's announcement represented a significant change in U.S. policy in the Persian Gulf, and it was entirely appropriate given the nature of the threats in the region. But that beneficial change will mean little if we merely replace a U.S. military presence in Saudi Arabia with an equally provocative and draining long-term presence in Iraq.

Before the start of the war, many people in the U.S. foreign policy community argued against an extended occupation of Iraq, recognizing that such a presence would be resented both by the Iraqis themselves and in the wider Arab and Muslim world. As a candidate for the presidency, George Bush, concerned about the United States being seen as an arrogant nation, questioned America's right to "go around the world and say, 'This is the way it's got to be.'"[5] And, yet, that is precisely the message conveyed by a U.S. military presence in Iraq.

Unfortunately, many political leaders and opinion makers, on both the left and the right, believe that the United States must "stay the course" and maintain the U.S. occupation for an extended period of time—although many of those people are vague about just how long that might be. Sen. John Kerry (D-MA) asserted that "extremists" in Iraq could not force a "premature withdrawal of U.S. troops" and could not shake the U.S. commitment "to help the Iraqis build a stable, peaceful and pluralistic society."[6] Noting President Bush's similar pledge to "complete the mission," the editors of USA Today opined that the "tricky dance" for both men involved "devising a revised exit plan that doesn't bog down U.S. forces in Iraq indefinitely or result in a premature pullout. . . . The challenge for Bush and Kerry is to head off pressure for an early pullout by finding a steady path for completing the job."[7]

A vocal minority goes one step further, arguing that U.S. troops must remain in Iraq indefinitely. Tom Donnelly of the American Enterprise Institute maintained that U.S. interests at stake in Iraq increased following Saddam Hussein's ouster. "The liberation of Iraq adds to the substantial list of U.S. interests in the region," wrote Donnelly in the Weekly Standard in May 2003, and he called for a "quasi-permanent American garrison in Iraq" to protect those interests.[8] When Rumsfeld asserted that the Pentagon was not planning to keep permanent bases in Iraq, avowed imperialist Max Boot of the Council on Foreign Relations exclaimed, "If they're not, they should be." Indeed, Boot called on USA Today readers to "get used to U.S. troops being deployed [in Iraq] for years, possibly decades, to come."[9]

Some people have used the rhetoric of democratization and political liberalization to justify a continued military occupation of Iraq. That sentiment flows from the belief that the creation of an Iraqi democracy is America's primary duty even after the fall of Saddam and the failure to find WMD. The general reasons for the support of Iraqi democracy are twofold: first, the humanitarian idea of democracy for democracy's sake and, second, the notion that democratic regimes tend not to threaten U.S. national security interests. According to AEI's Donnelly, the goal of the U.S. military presence in Iraq is "to secure a complete victory that will provide a foundation for Iraqi democracy."[10] Richard Perle, former chair of the Pentagon's influential Defense Policy Board, stated that, even after the liberation of Iraq from Saddam Hussein, the United States had a further obligation to liberate Iraqi society "from poverty, from corruption, and from the absence of a decent political life."[11]

Many supporters of a long-term military occupation believe that the United States has moral responsibility "for preserving the liberal international order," so that the fruits of liberal democratic society can be known in parts of the world hitherto isolated from the progress of civilization.[12] Iraq will be the political guinea pig for a new era of U.S.-led democratization and regime change. Two of the leading proponents of war with Iraq, the *New Republic*'s Lawrence Kaplan and William Kristol of the *Weekly Standard*, contend that the existence of the first Arab democracy in Iraq will "demonstrate the compatibility of our ideals and interests" to critics abroad and make the world a "safer and better place."[13] Reuel Marc Gerecht of the American Enterprise Institute went even further, proclaiming in an article in the *Weekly Standard* in December 2003, "The United States' standing in the Middle East and the world depends upon the transformation of American power into Iraqi democracy."[14] However, supporters of that point of view have noted that there are other U.S. interests involved in democratization, interests that lie beyond a simply humanitarian ethos. In a Project for the New American Century "Statement on Post-War Iraq," the signatories argued that the democratization of Iraq was not only desirable on a humanitarian level, but that it was "an objective of overriding strategic importance to the United States."[15] That was the point of view affirmed by President Bush in a nationally televised press conference in April 2004. "We're not going to leave. We're going to do the job," the president said. "A free Iraq in the midst of the Middle East is vital to future peace and security."[16]

That argument feeds into a broader critique, advanced since the events of September 11, 2001, in which support for a more pro-active U.S. defense policy is predicated on preempting the "forces that produce terror."[17] Toward this end, the argument goes, the United States must remain in Iraq long enough to ensure that a pro-Western, multiethnic, liberal democratic government is elected and remains in power. National Security Adviser Condoleezza Rice asserts that the creation of democracy in Iraq is a great cause that would transform the Middle East, similar to the defense of Western Europe from the Soviet Union after World War II. She declared that Americans, in concert with our allies, "must make a generational commitment to helping the people of the Middle East transform their region," because she admits that, "like the transformation of Europe, the transformation of the Middle East" will take "many years."[18]

The assertion that a prolonged U.S. occupation will produce a robust Iraqi democracy, a model that will then be exportable around the Middle East, is dubious at best. However, even if it were possible to export democracy at gunpoint, such a strategy would entail a much greater commitment than simply overthrowing unfriendly dictators; it would also require the formulation, and subsequent stabilization, of democratic institutions. As *New York Times* columnist Thomas Friedman put it, "America broke Iraq; now America owns Iraq, and it owns the primary responsibility for normalizing it."[19] Even many of those who questioned the legitimacy of the war have argued that the United States now has a responsibility to remain in Iraq for an extended period of time. House Minority Leader Nancy Pelosi, who voted against the Iraq war resolution, now says that the United States "must succeed in Iraq for our sake as well as that of the people of Iraq and their neighbors."[20] Sen. Edward Kennedy (D-MA) agrees. "It is essential to our national security," he declared in a recent statement, "to create a stable government in Iraq and prevent it from becoming a breeding ground for terrorists."[21]

The concern that Iraq could descend into chaos and become a "breeding ground for terrorists" was present well before the war, even among the most enthusiastic advocates of military action against Iraq. For example, Under Secretary of Defense Douglas Feith wondered aloud how the United States could establish a foundation "for the kind of . . . broad-based, representative government building on democratic institutions and the like. A government that will be humane to its own people and not a threat to its neighbors, not have WMD, [and] not support terrorism."[22]

Although Feith asserted that the U.S. objective was to "get the Iraqis running their own affairs as soon as possible" and that the United States is "not looking to occupy the country," the project that the United States is undertaking is unmistakably long term.[23] Donnelly points out that, even taking an optimistic view of Iraq's potential for creating a pluralistic political order and the rule of law, "there will still be a desire to protect the nascent Iraqi democracy in a nasty neighborhood."[24] That implies the need for a U.S. military presence in Iraq for not only the time it takes to *create* democratic, pluralist, political structures and liberal economic structures where they have not existed hitherto but also subsequent to their formation so as to ensure their stability and health. The difficulty was captured by an unnamed administration official quoted in the *New York Times*: "We're boxed in. We have a highly difficult set of issues to deal with here. We can't settle for just anything that gets us out of Iraq. . . . If we turn things over [on July 1, 2004] to whatever slapdash conglomeration that is out there . . . you could have a civil war in Iraq come next November."[25] Accordingly, *Newsweek*'s Fareed Zakaria calls for "candor about the costs of the occupation and our determination to stay," arguing that that "will send a signal to the world and, most important, to the Iraqi people that they will have a predictable, stable future."[26]

The president embraces the view that the war in Iraq is tied to the war against Al Qaeda by the broader goal of planting democracy in Iraq. President Bush delivered four major speeches in 2003 pledging to establish a democratic system in Iraq as the first step toward promoting liberal democracy in the entire Middle East. "Iraqi democracy will succeed—and that success will send forth the news, from Damascus to Tehran—that freedom can be the future of every nation," Bush stated in a speech delivered to the National Endowment for Democracy in Washington, DC, on November 6, 2003. "The establishment of a free Iraq at the heart of the Middle East will be a watershed event in the global democratic revolution," he predicted, stressing that the United States was not only preaching democracy in Iraq but also trying to build there a model for other Arab nations to follow.[27]

Although most Americans supported the war in Iraq out of concern that Iraq posed a threat to the United States (indeed, a poll taken in August 2003 found that 7 of 10 Americans still believed that Saddam Hussein had a hand in the September 11 attacks),[28] the Bush administration's broader goal of using regime change in Iraq as a vehicle for forcibly democratizing the entire Middle East was always there, under the surface. Bush had mentioned the spread of democracy in the Middle East as a justification for the invasion of Iraq in a speech before the American Enterprise Institute on the eve of the war in February 2003.[29]

Indeed, the enthusiasm with which President Bush has embraced "nation building" in Iraq, and the wider goal of promoting democracy throughout the Arab world, has intrigued those observers who recall that during the 2000 presidential campaign former Texas governor Bush stressed his commitment to a Realpolitik approach in advancing U.S. interests abroad and rejected the Wilsonian agenda of humanitarian military intervention championed by his predecessor Bill Clinton in the Balkans, Haiti, and Somalia.[30]

15

And yet, less than three years later, President George Bush had embarked on one of the most ambitious nation-building schemes in American history. Regardless of the original justifications for going to war, all indications are that the Bush administration expects to be in Iraq for a very, very long time. In January 2004 it was reported that the Pentagon was considering the appointment of a new four-star general to be stationed in Baghdad. That individual would be expected to operate independent of Central Command (CENTCOM), the current regional Commander-in-Chief (CINC). The creation of a new Middle East Command in Baghdad, complete with the support staff commensurate with a four-star CINC command, also reflects the Pentagon's belief that the military situation in Iraq and the wider Middle East–Near East region is far from settled.[31] Although the Pentagon did not confirm the reports, chairman of the Joint Chiefs of Staff Gen. Richard Myers conceded that it was "probably not unreasonable" to expect that troops would be in Iraq for decades.[32] Combine that military posture with the statements and actions of the State Department and other U.S. government agencies concerning the size and scope of the American diplomatic presence in Iraq. The United States is planning to create one of the largest U.S. diplomatic missions in the world in Baghdad, with a staff of more than 1,000.[33] All of those signs point to one conclusion: the United States intends to continue calling many (if not most) of the shots in Iraq long after the handover of political sovereignty.

None of the arguments for a continued military occupation is compelling. A long-term military presence in Iraq would be disastrous for the United States.

First of all, the continuing occupation of Iraq is counterproductive. It diverts attention and resources from the greatest threat facing the United States today: Al Qaeda and other anti-American terrorist organizations that wish to kill Americans. For the past year and a half, Iraq has monopolized America's attention. Everyone, from the military, the intelligence community, and the foreign policy apparatus, to the news media, the Washington think tanks, and of course the public itself, has been riveted by the spectacle of the invasion and occupation of Iraq. It is hardly surprising that too little attention has been paid to a number of tangible and far-reaching national security threats that have been festering during this period. Even more ominous, the U.S. military presence in Iraq has emboldened anti-American terrorists, serving as a vehicle for recruiting a whole new class of disgruntled men and women anxious to inflict harm on the United States.[34]

Second, a permanent military garrison in Iraq is not needed to protect vital U.S. interests, and the maintenance of such a troop presence will impose enormous costs and create a host of new headaches for the American taxpayers and the military alike. Those who favor maintaining a military presence in Iraq largely ignore the costs and risks associated with such a strategy. And yet, even conservative estimates of costs extend into the hundreds of billions of dollars. During a radio interview in June 2003, Lawrence Kaplan, senior editor at the *New Republic*, dismissed concerns about costs out of hand. Still, when pressed on specifics, Kaplan did not dispute that the occupation of Iraq alone would cost hundreds of billions of dollars. "I think that's a fair estimate," he said, but, he continued, "I don't think the most appropriate way of looking at this situation is through green eyeshades."[35]

It's true that the costs to our military can't be quantified by green-eyeshade-wearing accountants. The intangibles include the possibility that frequent exposure to risky and unappealing tours of duty in Iraq will drive down reenlistment rates and undermine recruitment for the all-volunteer force. Meanwhile, the costs of lives lost, and hundreds more forever disrupted by disabling injuries, are incalculable. From the beginning of operations in March 2003 to the end of April 2004, 764 men and women were killed and more than 3,800 injured in Iraq.[36]

Such costs are particularly tragic because they are so unnecessary. To argue that a permanent military presence in Iraq is needed to protect American security interests in the region is to ignore some of the most important lessons learned from the Iraq war. Such lessons, combined with data from similar operations conducted elsewhere around the globe since the end of the Cold War, demonstrate the American military's remarkable capacity for long-range power projection.

Just as there is no military or strategic need for forces in Iraq, there is no economic imperative for keeping troops there. The American military presence is not essential, and might even be detrimental, to ensuring access to Persian Gulf oil. Some people who favor a continued American troop presence in the Middle East may presume

17

that military pressure will dissuade hostile governments from refusing to sell oil to the United States. Others may contend that the presence of the U.S. military in Iraq is a stabilizing influence throughout the region. But U.S. policy in the Persian Gulf should not be based on the assumption that the region's energy resources will not make it to market absent the presence of U.S. troops. Oil is the principal source of revenue for the Persian Gulf countries; they could not withhold it from world markets without committing economic suicide.

Third, we have already noted that a U.S. military occupation of Iraq is counterproductive in terms of fighting Al Qaeda and anti-American terrorism. Such a presence is equally harmful in terms of the wider goal of fostering democracy in the country and the region. The argument that the U.S. military must protect and defend Iraqi democracy forgets or ignores that the primary justification for launching military action was the removal of Saddam Hussein from power and the elimination of Iraq's WMD. Our servicemen and servicewomen fulfilled their mission by separating Saddam Hussein from the instruments of power. And subsequent searches have failed to uncover the weapons stocks that Hussein was alleged to have been hiding. Hussein may have been the primary impediment to representative government in Iraq, but the removal of that impediment is merely a useful byproduct of the American military victory. The United States cannot ensure that the Iraqis will elect liberal democrats to represent them. The tasks of governing must be left to the Iraqi people.

Finally, the need for a prompt military withdrawal implies a willingness to accept a less-than-perfect outcome in Iraq. But that is precisely what policymaking entails. It requires our leaders to make choices—to prioritize essential needs, achievable objectives, and unattainable desires. To expect perfection in an imperfect world or, worse, to design our foreign policies around the belief that we can create a perfect world is to fall victim to the same types of utopian fantasies that have destroyed past civilizations.

The following chapters detail what the United States must do, and why, and lead to a single, unequivocal conclusion. The United States must refocus its attention on genuine threats, and we must reallocate our resources—military, diplomatic, intelligence gathering, and law enforcement—to the fight against anti-American terrorists. That must begin with an expeditious military withdrawal from Iraq.

2. The Occupation of Iraq Is Counterproductive to Addressing the Terror Threat

Having documented some of the leading objections to an expeditious withdrawal, we now turn to a more detailed discussion of the merits of such an exit. More than a year after the fall of Saddam's regime, and with the despised dictator himself behind bars, U.S. forces remain in Iraq with no plan for withdrawal. On the contrary, current plans call for retaining nearly 140,000 GIs in Iraq at least through the end of 2005.[37] Privately, military leaders anticipate that the same number of troops will remain in Iraq at least through the spring of 2007, and most expect a sizable military presence for at least the next decade. Determined foes subject those forces to regular attacks and also target Iraqis who cooperate with them. The risks that such sporadic attacks could quickly spiral into widespread opposition to the U.S. occupation were dramatically revealed in April 2004, when forces loyal to Shiite cleric Moqtada al-Sadr waged dozens of pitched battles with Coalition forces. Lest anyone believe the optimistic assertions of the White House and its ideological allies that the security situation in Iraq had measurably improved since Saddam's ouster, it is now obvious that U.S. military and civilian officials alike are involved in an intense conflict with determined foes, navigating the pitfalls inherent in attempting to manage complex ethnic, religious, and tribal issues.

President Bush argued that the war to depose Saddam Hussein was part of the wider war on terrorism. In the fall of 2002, the Bush administration billed its impending action against Iraq as a preemptive move to disarm Saddam of his purported stocks of WMD, citing a dire threat to national security. Before the UN General Assembly one year and one day after the events of September 11, 2001, President Bush declared that Saddam Hussein's regime posed "a grave and gathering danger."[38] Less than a month later, the president declared that Saddam's regime posed "a threat of unique urgency."[39] Those warnings appeared particularly compelling in the aftermath of September 11. Many Americans viewed a terrorist-supporting dictator who likely possessed WMD as a clear and present danger that needed to be neutralized.

The swift overthrow of Saddam Hussein's regime called into question the severity of the Iraqi threat and of Hussein's supposed ability to menace his neighbors. Those questions were amplified by the failure to locate Iraqi WMD. The Bush administration's reasons for the continued U.S. presence in Iraq then shifted, with a new emphasis on the democratization of the Middle East as the primary object of U.S. action in Iraq. The premise was that lack of democracy in the Middle East, combined with the ongoing Israeli-Palestinian dispute, contributed to global terror. Those broader issues, beyond Saddam's purported threat to the United States, became part of the U.S.-led war on terrorism. "With no WMD having been unearthed thus far in Iraq, and with the costs of the war in lives and dollars soaring, the president felt he needed a new rationale," speculated Thomas Friedman. "And so he focused on the democratization argument."[40]

By late summer and early fall of 2003, as Iraq was gripped by a fierce anti-American insurgency, the rationale for the war shifted again. In a speech in September 2003, President Bush sought to conflate the Iraq occupation with the continued conflict in Afghanistan by claiming that "the surest way to avoid attacks on our own people is to engage the enemy where he lives and plans." "We are fighting that enemy in Iraq and Afghanistan today," the president assured his audience, "so that we do not meet him again on our own streets, in our own cities." Iraq, the president said, was now "the central front" in the war on terror.[41]

If Iraq had indeed become the central front in the terror war, then that was an entirely new development. A survey of the annual "Patterns of Global Terrorism" published by the U.S. Department of State does not support such a contention. For example, the State Department's report for the year 2000 states, "The [Iraqi] regime has not attempted an anti-Western terrorist attack since its failed plot to assassinate former President Bush in 1993 in Kuwait."[42] Some inactive and insignificant terrorist groups such as the 15 May Organization and the Arab Liberation Front maintained offices in Iraq.

There was no mention, however, of any links between the Iraqi regime and Al Qaeda or any other terrorist group that was a threat to the United States.

On the other hand, the same report states that Sudan "continued to be used as a safe haven by members of various groups, including associates of Usama Bin Ladin's al-Qaida organization." The report also goes into considerable detail on the links between Pakistan's military government and a number of terrorist groups including Lashkar-e-Tayyiba, Harakat ul-Mujahidin, and Jaish-e-Mohammed, all of which have been closely linked to Al Qaeda.[43]

Thus, Iraq was hardly a "central front" in the war on terror before the March 2003 U.S. invasion. Accepting the president's assertion that it is now leads one to suspect that the U.S. invasion and occupation are responsible for making it so.

Saddam Hussein, Al Qaeda, and September 11

The evidence linking Saddam Hussein's regime to Al Qaeda has always been tenuous at best. It has proved harder still to tie Hussein to the September 11 attacks, even as the president's rhetoric has fueled American misperceptions of a link. In his speech on May 1, 2003, declaring the end of major combat in Iraq, President Bush explicitly associated the war in Iraq with the attacks: "The battle of Iraq is one victory in a war on terror that began on September 11, 2001." And yet, administration officials have repeatedly admitted that they have found no evidence linking Hussein to the September 11 attacks. Deputy Defense Secretary Paul Wolfowitz conceded that he didn't "believe that the evidence was there to suggest that Iraq had played a direct role in 9/11."[44] On the same day Secretary Rumsfeld said that he had no reason to believe that Hussein was involved, the president was even more categorical, telling a group of lawmakers meeting with him at the White House, "No, we've had no evidence that Saddam Hussein was involved in September the 11th."[45]

Vice President Cheney appears to cling to the notion that proof of such a linkage will eventually be found, however. Referring to a supposed meeting between 9/11 ringleader Mohammed Atta and an Iraqi intelligence officer in Prague in April 2000, Cheney said in late 2001 that it was "pretty well confirmed" that such a meeting took place. He backed off slightly from that assertion in September

2003, saying only that "we just don't know" whether the allegations were true.[46]

In fact, the stories of the Prague meeting have been disputed by numerous sources. As early as October 2002, long before the planned invasion of Iraq, Czech president Václav Havel informed senior Bush administration officials that Czech domestic intelligence had found no evidence to substantiate the claim. Separately, Czech security officials noted that they had never seen evidence that Iraqi intelligence agents in Prague were in any way involved in terrorist activity.[47] "An FBI investigation concluded that Atta was apparently in Florida at the time of the alleged meeting," the *Washington Post* reported, "and the CIA has always doubted it took place."[48]

Rohan Gunaratna, a renowned terrorism expert, found no Iraq–Al Qaeda link after poring over tens of thousands of documents recovered from Al Qaeda detainees and debriefing several of those detainees.[49] On the contrary, he reported that Al Qaeda regarded Saddam Hussein as an infidel who had ruled over a secular Iraq. Similarly, European intelligence officers and law enforcement experts dismiss claims of an Iraq–Al Qaeda link. The *Los Angeles Times* reported in November 2002 that it was hard to find anyone even in the British government, a loyal ally in the war against Hussein, making the case that Al Qaeda and the Iraqi regime were close allies.[50]

Undaunted, the administration proceeded with its plans to go to war. Just before the invasion, Khalid Sheikh Mohammed, the Al Qaeda figure captured a few weeks before the March 2003 Iraq invasion, told interrogators that the terrorist group rejected links with Saddam Hussein's corrupt and secular regime.[51]

Instead of forging any kind of alliance with a secular ruler whom he despised, Osama bin Laden has cynically used anger and resentment toward the U.S. treatment of Iraqi civilians, including the 12 years of sanctions following the first Gulf War, as a recruiting tool for his organization. Still, very few Iraqis identified with bin Laden's cause prior to the U.S. invasion. None of the 19 September 11 hijackers was an Iraqi national. None of the dozens of other attacks attributed to Al Qaeda during the past decade has been tied to Iraqi citizens.

Meanwhile, author Laurie Mylroie's contention that Ramzi Yousef, the mastermind behind the 1993 World Trade Center bombing, was an Iraqi intelligence agent has been thoroughly refuted. As terrorism expert Peter Bergen points out in a devastating article that systematically deconstructs all of Mylroie's specious claims, "The Joint Terrorism Task Force in New York, the F.B.I, the U.S. Attorney's office in the Southern District of New York, the C.I.A., the N.S.C, and the State Department had all found no evidence implicating the Iraqi government in the first Trade Center attack."[52] Richard Clarke's account of the anti-terrorism efforts of the Clinton and both Bush administrations confirms that extraordinary efforts on the part of Deputy Secretary of Defense Wolfowitz to prove Mylroie's theories were unavailing. "More than anyone in the Clinton administration," Clarke writes, "I wanted an excuse to eliminate the Saddam Hussein regime. . . . More than anyone, I *wanted* the World Trade Center attack to be an Iraqi operation so we could justify reopening the war with Iraq—but there was no good evidence leading to Baghdad's culpability."[53]

Since Saddam's ouster, experts have found no compelling links between his government and Al Qaeda. Jason Burke, a British investigative reporter who has done extensive research on Islamic extremism in Pakistan and Afghanistan, also concludes that no evidence exists to link Saddam Hussein and Al Qaeda.[54] The only purportedly Al Qaeda–affiliated terror group known to have operated in Iraq before the March 2003 U.S.-led invasion was Ansar-al-Islam; however, Burke asserts that the loose organization associated with the Jordanian militant Abu Masub al-Zarqawi was in many ways a competitor to bin Laden's Al Qaeda. Indeed, in his book on Al Qaeda, Burke notes that some members of Ansar-al-Islam were individuals who had "no broader agenda beyond Kurdistan," and still others "did not care for bin Laden or his vision of an international struggle. It did not interest them at all." And even if the two groups shared some common objectives, Ansar-al-Islam operated in the Kurdish regions of Iraq that had not been under Saddam's control since 1991.[55] Therefore, it is difficult to understand how they can serve as evidence of a Saddam–Al Qaeda "link."

In an October 2003 memo, Douglas Feith repeated allegations of a link between Saddam Hussein's regime and Al Qaeda. However, critics charged that the conclusions were drawn from unverified and questionable intelligence and were based on a selective reading of reports, omitting information that would have contradicted those conclusions.[56] Subsequent news reports have revealed that the Iraqi exile group the Iraqi National Congress had a hand in disseminating misleading and inaccurate reports pertaining to Iraq.[57] In an interview with the *Telegraph* (London) INC leader Ahmed Chalabi shrugged off the accusations. "We are heroes in error," he said, "What was said before is not important."[58]

Now, however, following the invasion and occupation of Iraq, we have witnessed a spate of attacks on U.S. and Coalition forces and against Iraqis willing to cooperate with occupation authorities. Many of those attacks have been tied to disaffected former Baath Party officials and to Iraqi nationalists opposed to the occupation, but a number appear to have been staged by terrorists at least loosely affiliated with Al Qaeda.[59] In short, Iraq was never before a hotbed of terrorism, but it now has become a magnet for such activity.

When Americans shifted attention and resources to Iraq, the task of eliminating Al Qaeda and the Taliban was largely delegated to Pakistani Gen. Pervez Musharraf's weak and duplicitous regime.[60] By fall 2002, the Taliban was reconstituting its forces, and many Al Qaeda members had dispersed. The terrorist groups in eastern Afghanistan and western Pakistan that provide shelter and sanctuary to bin Laden's forces continued their activities, including collecting funds for jihad and running terrorist camps. From across the globe, financial support continued to flow to Al Qaeda. A United Nations report in August 2002 found that only a small percentage of money flowing into global jihad was traceable.[61]

A number of experts agree that Iraq has diverted resources from the fight against Al Qaeda. Flynt Leverett, a former CIA analyst and Middle East specialist on the Bush National Security Council, said that Arabic-speaking Special Forces personnel and CIA officers were pulled out of Afghanistan in March 2002 to prepare for the Iraq invasion. Pat Lang, former head of Middle East and South Asia intelligence at the Defense Intelligence Agency, pointed out, "When you commit as much time and attention and resources as we did in Iraq, . . . then you subtract what you could commit to the war on terrorism."[62]

Current intelligence officials, while denying that Iraq has had a negative effect on the war on terror, acknowledge that there has been a shortage of experts and that the intelligence community is struggling to meet the challenge. According to a report in the *Los Angeles Times*, current and former intelligence officers said the agency "was confronting one of the most difficult challenges in its history." "I think they're just sucking wind," said one former officer.[63] We may never know the extent to which the quality of intelligence collection and analysis has suffered in the process.

In February 2004, the Pentagon reported that a special task force created to hunt for senior Iraqi insurgents had redirected its attention to bin Laden and other senior Taliban and Al Qaeda officials. Task Force 121, which included personnel from the Army's Delta Force and the Navy SEALs, accompanied the unit from 4th Infantry Division that captured Saddam Hussein on December 13, 2003.[64] Although that shift was good news, subsequent unrest in Iraq threatens to draw those forces back into Iraq, away from the anti–Al Qaeda hunt.

Iraq, Terrorism, and the WMD Threat

The prospect that anti-American terrorists could get nuclear weapons is perhaps the greatest threat to U.S. national security. The Bush administration has advanced the notion that its action against Hussein's Iraq will deter other nations that may be in the process of developing nuclear weapons programs. Pointing to Libya's decision to end its WMD program, President Bush in his January 2004 State of the Union speech stated that "for diplomacy to be effective, words must be credible, and no one can now doubt the word of America."[65] The president implied that the fate of the Iraqi regime persuaded Libyan dictator Moammar Gaddafi to discard his nuclear ambitions. The administration has made similar suggestions with respect to Iran and North Korea.

It is possible that the U.S. action in Iraq has made some nations rethink their plans for acquiring WMD. Nuclear proliferation expert Joseph Cirincione wonders, however, whether the United States has "been able to work out deals with Iran and Libya, two of the most difficult regimes in the world, because [those countries] feared that they were next in the Bush administration's cross hairs, or because the United States is so tied down in Iraq that the administration finds it necessary to seek diplomatic solutions?"[66] Cirincione believes the latter, arguing that Iran's willingness to negotiate has much more to do with engagement by European nations than with American belligerence. In fact, Iran may yet be hedging its bets against future U.S. threats, and it is far from clear that it has indeed given up its nuclear program.[67] Meanwhile, former U.S. senator Gary Hart shed further light on Libya's apparent about-face in a *Washington Post* op-ed in January 2004. Hart detailed how Gaddafi's regime was willing to negotiate its WMD program away more than a decade ago.[68] Flynt Leverett, a former official at the National Security Council and a Middle East expert at the Brookings Institution, confirms that the Libyan move followed years of negotiations and that the specific deal concerning its WMD program was agreed to before the start of the Iraq war.[69]

In addition, North Korea, an avowed member of the nuclear club, has not stepped back from its nuclear brinkmanship. While the United States invaded Iraq, drove Saddam into hiding, and finally captured him, North Korea continued its nuclear program. In January 2004, a top North Korean official told a group of Americans invited to visit the North's nuclear facilities, "Time's not on your side, as time goes by, we are increasing our arsenal."[70] Although its claims to possess actual nuclear weapons have not been verified, the Democratic People's Republic of Korea appears to have reprocessed thousands of spent fuel rods during the past year, sufficient for the production of several nuclear bombs.[71]

Almost a year after America waged preemptive war against Iraq to rid the world of a regime purported to possess WMD, the advertised gains of a belligerent strategy have not materialized. There is a growing perception around the world that possession of such weapons may be the only way to deter American belligerence. North Korea and Iran have either brazenly continued to expand their nuclear programs or have bought time through negotiation for future development of nuclear weapons. In May 2003 a U.S. congressional delegation visited North Korea. According to Curt Weldon, a Republican representative from Pennsylvania who headed the delegation, North Korea said that it was developing its nuclear weapons as "a response to what they saw happened [sic] in Iraq, with the U.S. removing Saddam Hussein from power."[72] The leaders there, and possibly in Iran as well, may have determined that Iraq's quick collapse derived from its lack of WMD. The Iraq war has given other nations new incentives to acquire the deterrent that Iraq lacked.

Many people around the globe suspect that the Iraqi WMD threat was overplayed all along. Wolfowitz suggested that policymakers "settled on the one issue that everyone could agree on which was weapons of mass destruction as the core reason" for going to war.[73] Both the White House and Tony Blair's government in the United Kingdom have established special commissions to investigate why the prewar intelligence on Iraq's WMD programs was so faulty.

Although it is proper to review history to glean lessons for the future, policy should be focused on the here and now. If indeed the American invasion of Iraq was aimed at overthrowing Saddam and separating him from his WMD arsenal, then that job is done. Saddam Hussein is in custody, and, even accepting the increasingly dubious assumption that he recently had his hands on terror weapons, he cannot possibly deploy such weapons from a jail cell. Much of the U.S. force looking for WMDs has been withdrawn from Iraq or reassigned to other missions. If the United States wants the rest of the world to believe that the Iraqi invasion was a defensive war aimed at reducing the threat posed by WMD, it should consider its job done and end the occupation as soon as possible.

Instead, by continuing with the military occupation of Iraq, the United States plays into suspicions that its actions were somehow driven by a desire to negotiate lucrative reconstruction contracts, gain control over oil, or achieve other imperial designs. That perception, however unfair, directly aids Al Qaeda and other anti-American terrorists who will use specious accusations of American perfidy to attract new recruits.[74]

The continued U.S. occupation of Iraq also serves to distract Americans from an even bigger threat. While America has been focused on the Iraq occupation, the proliferation of Pakistani nuclear technology to Iran, North Korea, Libya, and possibly Saudi Arabia has been going on "under the radar." The recent revelations about Iran's and Libya's nuclear programs have shown that Pakistani centrifuge technology was leaked to both nations. Pakistani nuclear technology was also shipped to North Korea as recently as last year.[75]

The presence of U.S. forces in Iraq does not contribute measurably to the elimination of the WMD threat. On the contrary, the failure to locate such a threat emanating from Iraq sends troubling signals about U.S. intentions to many nations. An acknowledgement that WMD have not been found in Iraq, and a subsequent end to the occupation along with a more serious approach to the actual WMD dangers around the world, is more likely to secure peace for Americans than the current policy that ignores the worst threats.

Diversion and Distraction

The U.S.-led invasion and occupation of Iraq undermine the fight against radical Islamic terrorists. Instead of weakening such groups, it aids bin Laden in his quest to marshal the various and competing Islamic factions around the world in a common war against the West. President Bush has repeatedly stated that the war on terrorism is not a war on Islam. And yet, by characterizing the war in Iraq as part of the wider war on terrorism, the president may inadvertently foment the very clash of civilizations he wishes to avoid.

Al Qaeda terrorists seized upon the U.S. military presence in Saudi Arabia as a twisted justification for their acts of violence, beginning in the mid-1990s. Those avowed enemies of the West have now been joined by new groups, incensed by the presence of U.S. troops in and near Muslim holy sites in Iraq. They seethe at inadvertent transgressions of Islamic faith and custom. Non-Arab Muslims, even those who are unsympathetic to bin Laden's radical interpretation of Islamic law, perceive the presence of American forces in Baghdad, once the capital of the Islamic caliphate, as a humiliating affront to Islam; many Arabs view the American military presence in that historic city, long a center of Arab culture, as an insult to all Arabs.

Indeed, Ibrahim M. Abu-Rabi, professor of Islamic studies and codirector of the Macdonald Center for the Study of Islam and Christian-Muslim relations at Hartford Seminary, predicted that "the American occupation of Iraq is certainly going to enhance the position of extremist Islamist movements in the Muslim world."[76] That danger was recognized by Wolfowitz, who admitted in late February 2003, before the commencement of Operation Iraqi Freedom, that anger at American pressure on Iraq and resentment over the stationing of U.S. forces in Saudi Arabia had "been Osama bin Laden's principal recruiting device."[77] He opined that the removal of U.S. troops from the kingdom would have positive effects throughout the region. "Just lifting that burden from the Saudis is itself going to open the door" to a more peaceful Middle East, Wolfowitz told an interviewer in the spring of 2003.[78]

Looking ahead to the post-Hussein period, Wolfowitz implied that the removal of Hussein would enable the United States to withdraw troops from the region. "I can't imagine anyone here wanting to . . . be there for another 12 years to continue helping recruit terrorists."[79] And yet Pentagon plans seem to call for a long-term military presence in Iraq. In early May 2004, Defense Department officials reported that they expected to keep nearly 140,000 troops in Iraq at least through the end of 2005.[80] Earlier, military leaders had confided that they expected a sizable U.S. force to remain in Iraq for at least a decade. Gen. Richard Myers was even more blunt, telling reporters in April 2004 that a U.S. troop presence in Iraq might extend for decades.[81]

Bogged down in a long-term military occupation in Iraq, America faces the prospect of having to combat a perpetually increasing number of new enemies, even as tremendous resources are already being expended to fight existing enemies. Jeffrey Record, a professor at the U.S. Air Force's Air War College, warns that the "global war on terrorism as currently defined and waged is dangerously indiscriminate and ambitious" and "strategically unfocused."[82]

Fears of U.S. strategic overstretch in the global war on terrorism, and of the U.S. occupation playing into bin Laden's strategy for recruiting new followers, are well-founded. According to a "senior intelligence official" interviewed by the *Washington Post*, Islamic military organizations in North Africa and Southeast Asia, which were previously focused on overthrowing local governments, "have been caught by bin Laden's vision, and poisoned by it." Claiming that the United States was now a target for those disparate groups, the unnamed official explained, "That is one manifestation of how bin Laden's views are expanding well beyond Iraq."[83]

And although the president has argued that the war in Iraq has severely weakened the forces of global terrorism, a December 2003 report in *Janes Intelligence Digest* found that "Al Qaeda and its affiliates continue to operate despite sanctions and travel bans" and that the group is continuing to collect funds from wealthy donors, criminal enterprises, and the illegal narcotics trade.[84] In testimony before Congress in late February 2004, CIA director George Tenet categorically reaffirmed that Al Qaeda posed a threat and that the terrorist network retained the ability to launch "catastrophic attacks" against the United States. Appearing alongside Tenet, FBI director Robert Mueller warned of attacks on subways and bridges in major cities and speculated that "Al Qaeda will revisit missed targets until they succeed." Vice Adm. Lowell Jacoby, director of the Defense Intelligence Agency, explained that attacks with portable, shoulder-fired missiles against civilian aircraft were a significant concern for intelligence and law enforcement officials.[85]

A prolonged U.S. military presence in Iraq is an open invitation for a steady buildup of grassroots Muslim anger. That anger is certain to converge on the United States, all of which plays further into bin Laden's evil designs. New terrorist networks are forming all over the globe. Active recruitment by groups sharing the Al Qaeda philosophy is being reported not only in Muslim-majority nations but also across Europe, including Italy, France, Britain, and Spain.

The bombings of several commuter trains in Spain on March 11, 2004, were originally attributed to the Basque separatist group ETA, but when the shadowy group Brigade of Abu Hafs al-Masri sent an e-mail to an Arabic newspaper based in London, attention focused on the possibility that Islamic terrorists had had a hand in the attacks. Spanish authorities subsequently identified six Moroccans who were believed to have carried out the attacks. One of those suspects, Jamal Zougam, was alleged to have ties to Salatin Jihadin, the group responsible for bombings in Casablanca in May 2003 that claimed the lives of 45 people. The attacks raise the specter of domestic terrorist groups making common cause with transnational entities such as Al Qaeda and posing an entirely new and deadly threat throughout Europe and beyond. Peter Beaumont and Anthony Barnett of the *Guardian* report that "dormant networks that once recruited and fed fighters into Afghanistan have" since the war in Iraq "been reactivated and reorganised for a new global jihad aimed at the U.S. and its allies."[86]

How the Occupation Feeds Global Jihad

There is an understandable impulse to want to prevent the preachers of radical Islamic ideology from recruiting would-be terrorists who may then perpetrate attacks, but the admonition to medical doctors seems more applicable: *primum non nocere* (first do no harm). If our counterterrorism efforts are actually contributing to a worsening perception of the United States by a growing number of Muslims, and if that leads to hostility toward the United States, then we have adopted a losing strategy. On at least one level, Rumsfeld himself seemed to recognize that concern. In a confidential memorandum to his staff, Rumsfeld asked, perhaps rhetorically, "Are we winning or losing the Global War on Terror?" and "Are we capturing, killing or deterring and dissuading more terrorists every day than the madrassas and the radical clerics are recruiting, training and deploying against us?" Worried that the United States lacked "metrics" to measure success or failure, Rumsfeld conceded, "We are having mixed results with Al Qaida" and "we are just getting started" with Ansar Al-Islam. Accordingly, he wondered whether the United States needed "to fashion a broad, integrated plan to stop the next generation of terrorists."[87]

A winning strategy must begin with a better understanding of the nature of the threat and then proceed to realistic measures for monitoring and containing the threat. The invasion and subsequent occupation of Iraq are based on the premise that U.S.-led regime change in the Arab world will undermine bin Laden's radical ideology. But regime change (or decapitation, the popular term used in the targeting of Saddam during the invasion) does not cure the underlying ideology of radical Islam. On the contrary, such action can instead focus the energies and wrath of the subscribers to that ideology on the United States and its allies. That will be particularly true if the regime change is based on dubious national security justifications.

In the 1980s and 1990s, several Islamic groups, including bin Laden's Al Qaeda, followed in the path laid out by scholars such as Syed Qutb of the Egyptian Muslim Brotherhood and his associate Abdallah Azzam. Those groups battled their respective regional authorities whom they perceived as oppressors. Bin Laden, however, diverged from that approach by redirecting his anger away from the corrupt regime of the House of Saud and toward the United States. He focused particular attention on the presence of U.S. troops in Saudi Arabia after the first Persian Gulf War. The September 11, 2001, attacks, as well as earlier attacks on U.S. embassies in Africa in 1998 and on the USS *Cole* in 2000, constituted a series of opening strikes in his war on the United States.

When bin Laden created the International Islamic Front in 1998, only a few groups from Egypt, Pakistan, and Bangladesh signed up to fight in the redirected crusade.[88] The Iraq invasion and the subsequent occupation, however, have changed the equation. Intense Muslim resentment of the United States is only reinforced by the perception that the U.S. invasion was motivated by greed, by a desire to control Iraq's oil resources, for construction profits for companies connected to the Bush administration, or even for a wholesale re-colonization of Iraq. Although such accusations might seem absurd on their face, even inconsequential stories, such as the reports of price gouging by U.S. subcontractors, are important not just for their scandalous import within the United States but because they seem to confirm in the minds of Muslims around the globe the malicious intentions of the United States.

A series of events in early April 2004 precipitated an intensification and widening of the Iraqi insurgency, which threatens to accelerate the buildup of anti-American sentiment among Muslims and could ultimately inspire terrorists wedded to Al Qaeda's philosophy to redouble their efforts. The events were triggered when the U.S.-led occupation authorities shut down a newspaper published by Shiite cleric Moqtada al-Sadr and later attempted to serve a warrant for his arrest. Al-Sadr's newspaper had been publishing inflammatory articles urging readers to resist the U.S. occupation, and the relatively junior cleric has a considerable following in Baghdad and some cities and towns in southern Iraq. Al-Sadr's followers, including his armed militia, the Mahdi Army, responded to Coalition pressure on al-Sadr by carrying out attacks on U.S.-led Coalition forces and taking over key installations in several Iraqi cities. That largely Shiite uprising took U.S. officials by surprise, as Shiites had been systematically repressed by Hussein's regime and had been generally supportive of U.S. aims.

During the same time, clashes erupted between U.S. Marines and largely Sunni insurgents in Fallujah. Sporadic fighting culminated in the ghastly killing and mutilation of several American contractors and was followed by a U.S. military assault on the town. The attacks on Sadr's followers and on the people of Fallujah fed into one other, with the images of Iraqi casualties inflaming anti-American sentiments across the nation. More than a hundred American troops, and a number of civilian contractors, were killed during this period. But the losses also extended to declining American prestige as anti-U.S. insurgents at least temporarily gained control of large areas in many towns across the nation, and the American military was forced to call a temporary ceasefire in Fallujah as reports of hundreds of Iraqi civilian casualties resonated in the region.

Soon after the events of early April, the leaders of two of America's closest regional allies, President Hosni Mubarak of Egypt and King Abdullah of Jordan, expressed grave concerns about intensifying animosity toward the United States across the region. On April 20,

2004, Mubarak said, "After what has happened in Iraq, there is unprecedented hatred and the Americans know it." "The despair and feeling of injustice are not going to be limited to our region alone," he warned.[89] A few days earlier, Jordan's King Abdullah expressed similar sentiments. During a question and answer session following his speech to the Commonwealth Club in San Francisco, Abdullah explained that images of "an American tank pointing at Iraqi citizens . . . [are] creating . . . in the Middle East . . . some sort of animosity that I never felt or heard about towards the United States."[90]

Terrorism expert Rohan Gunaratna fears that such intensifying animosity could translate into an increased threat of terrorism. "Iraq is the new land of jihad and the events there are having a profound impact on the Islamic movements and Muslim societies worldwide," Gunaratna reports, and he worries that "Iraq was now providing the inspiration for a new generation of terrorists."[91]

Even before the operations in Fallujah and the crackdown on al-Sadr's followers, the strategy for defusing anti-American resentment in Iraq seems to have been the incarceration of supposed terrorists and would-be terrorists. Many Iraqis have been detained by occupation authorities without charges being brought against them, inviting comparisons, however unfair, with the abuses of Saddam's regime and condemnation by international human rights groups.[92] Those comparisons seemed only more plausible with the revelation of prisoner abuse in the Abu Ghraib prison.

The rhetoric used in April 2004 against U.S. occupation forces is eerily similar to that used in the past in Iraq. Some Iraqis recalled how the slogan "No more Shiites after today" was painted on the barrels of Iraqi tanks dispatched in 1991 to crush a nascent Shiite rebellion. After the fall of Saddam, some Shiites turned that around on their Sunni oppressors with slogans in Shiite-dominated cities in southern Iraq declaring "No Baathists after today." In a stark demonstration of the extent to which traditional animosities among Iraq's religious and ethnic groups have been subsumed beneath common hostility toward American and Coalition forces, *Washington Post* reporters noticed, after a week of violence concentrated against the city of Fallujah, a sign declaring "No more occupation after today."[93] A poll taken in late March and early April 2004, before much of the fighting that took place in April and before the Abu

Ghraib scandal, found that 57 percent of Iraqis wanted the occupa-
tion to end immediately, and 67 percent believed that attacks against
U.S. forces in Iraq were justified at least some of the time.[94] An earlier
ABC news poll found that nearly half of all Iraqi Arabs surveyed
believed that the U.S. invasion was wrong and that it humiliated
Iraq.[95]

The problem of rising popular opposition is unique to neither Iraq
nor the U.S. military's tactics there. Counterinsurgency operations
necessitate the use of force against suspected insurgent hideouts,
raising the risk of collateral casualties among innocent Iraqis. Images
of those attacks, of destroyed buildings, and of dead and wounded
Iraqis are quickly amplified and broadcast to the Arab and Muslim
worlds by global media outlets such as Al Jazeera and Al Arabiya.
Two Al Jazeera headlines from October 2003—"U.S. Soldiers Trigger
Happy in Iraq" and "U.S. Occupiers Compared to Mongol Looters"—point to the public relations problem occupying armies face.[96]

Rising hostility toward the United States is not limited to Iraq. Two
polls conducted around the one-year anniversary of the beginning of
the war, but before the events of April and May 2004 that saw
widespread violence throughout much of Iraq, confirm the negative
effects that the occupation has already had on popular perceptions
of the United States. According to pollsters at the Pew Research
Center, "A year after the war in Iraq, discontent with America and
its policies has intensified rather than diminished." The poll shows
that large percentages of Pakistanis, Jordanians, and Moroccans view
Osama bin Laden favorably. Pew researchers also found that "over-
whelming majorities in Jordan and Morocco believe suicide attacks
against Americans and other Westerners in Iraq are justifiable."
Even in relatively liberal Turkey, 31 percent of those polled believe
that the attacks are justified.[97]

Whereas the teachings of Taimiya, Qutb, and Azzam once found
favor with only a small subset of the followers of Islam, these and
other polls show that bin Laden's struggle against the United States
now resonates with tens of millions of Muslims. The danger posed
by such resonance increases as the American occupation of Iraq
continues and images of humiliation and oppression are broadcast
around the globe.

3. A Long-Term Military Occupation Is Burdensome, Risky, and Ultimately Unsustainable

The American military occupation of Iraq distracts our attention from Al Qaeda and facilitates the recruitment of a new class of anti-American terrorists. Furthermore, U.S. forces must leave Iraq because it will be ruinously expensive—in terms of both dollars and lives—to stay. The occupation exposes our forces to intolerable risks. And those burdens and risks threaten to weaken the all-volunteer force, rendering it less capable of waging necessary wars in the future. The end result would be a diminution of America's ability to deter and defeat challengers to our vital security interests.

Dollars and Cents

Since the end of the first Gulf War, the United States has maintained a sizable military presence in the Persian Gulf region. More than 20,000 Americans were stationed near Iraq at the end of 2001, before the buildup for Operation Iraqi Freedom began.[98] The direct monetary costs of maintaining that presence were substantial. Deputy Secretary of Defense Paul Wolfowitz estimated that operations against Iraq in the 12 years since the end of the first Gulf War cost $30 billion; but that figure was only for Iraq, in particular the policing of the northern and southern no-fly zones, and therefore underestimated the total cost of all forces in the region. More complete estimates place the costs of U.S. troops in the Persian Gulf at at least 10 times that amount. In 1997 Graham Fuller and Ian Lesser of the RAND Corporation estimated that the U.S. presence cost taxpayers between $30 billion and $60 billion annually. Separately, Earl Ravenal, professor emeritus of the Georgetown University School of Foreign Service, estimated that the United States spent $50 billion a year to maintain its commitment to police the Gulf region.[99]

The cost of maintaining that force increased dramatically in 2002 and early 2003, as the U.S. military presence ballooned from 24,000 to more than 225,000 in preparation for war. Rough estimates of those costs may be derived from the Bush administration's two supplemental defense appropriation requests. The first, submitted in March 2003, totaled $74.7 billion and included $62.6 billion specifically earmarked for military operations.[100] Then, in August 2003, the administration returned with yet another supplemental request, this one for $87 billion, of which $51 billion was specifically for the military.[101]

The supplemental requests in 2003 covered combat operations as well as occupation duties. The cost of merely maintaining forces in Iraq during most of 2003 averaged nearly $4 billion per month.[102] During congressional testimony in April 2004, Deputy Defense Secretary Wolfowitz admitted that, as of January 2004, monthly operating costs in Iraq stood at $4.7 billion, and he expected those costs to rise in the months ahead, given an increase in the number of troops in the country. Gen. Richard Myers, chairman of the Joint Chiefs of Staff, agreed, admitting that intense combat, an increase in troop levels, and the need to replace or repair damaged equipment were "going to cost us more money."[103] Those are incremental costs, over and above what the U.S. government would be spending to maintain the same forces in the United States. The true costs of a long-term U.S. military presence in Iraq must be extrapolated from the overall defense budget. The Bush administration requested $400.5 billion for the Defense Department for fiscal year 2004, a staggering figure that seems all the more imposing considering that that amount did not include the cost of military operations in Iraq.[104] Incredibly, the administration refused initially to budget for the occupation and was planning instead to request a supplemental appropriation after the November election. But the White House succumbed to congressional pressure in May and submitted a supplemental request for $25 billion to fund military operations in both Iraq and Afghanistan.[105]

The United States already spends more on its military than all of the leading developed nations of the world, combined. If current trends continue, the United States will spend more than all of the rest of the planet by 2007. In an era of burdensome government spending, stifling taxation, and expanding deficits, Washington should be looking for ways to economize. Limiting the size and scope of our military would be a good place to start. Absent a firm commitment to substantially reduce, and in short order eliminate, the U.S. military garrison in Iraq, such economies will be impossible to achieve.

Squeezing the All-Volunteer Force

The solution to the problem, so far, is primarily to impose greater and greater burdens on our men and women in uniform. This, too, is unsustainable. The Bush administration should be reducing the number of missions that our armed forces are expected to complete. Instead, the administration keeps adding to the military's already-long to-do list. The true costs of a U.S. military occupation of Iraq must therefore also include the known and projected stresses that such an operation places on our all-volunteer force.

Military planners are always mindful of the pace at which operations are conducted and the frequency with which our troops are shifted from mission to mission and place to place. Ending the U.S. military occupation of Iraq would go a long way toward reducing the operational tempo (or op tempo, for short) for our forces. Relieving op tempo burdens will reduce the unseen and immeasurable hardships for our troops, including family separation, and may help to avert future recruitment and retention problems.

The Army plans to expand beyond its statutory limit of 480,000 personnel for the foreseeable future, and Congress appears ready to raise the limit still further. Most of the additional troops are slated for occupation duties in Iraq.[106] At the high point of the military buildup in support of the Iraq War, the total force, including Navy and Marine Corps personnel on board ships, numbered more than 225,000. The occupation force is projected to number nearly 140,000, at least through 2005, with later reductions contingent upon improvements in the security situation.[107] U.S. troop reductions are therefore highly dependent on the contribution of other forces, Iraqi or foreign. In the meantime, new U.S. troops are being introduced into the dangerous Iraqi theater every day. The troop rotation conducted in spring 2004 was the largest such operation ever attempted in America's history. An estimated 40 percent of the new arrivals were drawn from the ranks of the National Guard and Reserves.[108]

The strains on the Guard and Reserves continue a pattern that began under President Clinton in the 1990s. Reserve personnel are deployed at military installations worldwide, in support of missions in Bosnia and Kosovo, for example. Since the September 11 attacks, 300,000 National Guard personnel have been called up at one time or another.[109] At least 155,000 reservists have been activated.[110] While they are on active duty, those individuals are away from civilian jobs and therefore unable to contribute to the recovery of the domestic economy. Meanwhile, state and local officials worry about their ability to deal with natural disasters and other emergencies, given that as many as half of their forces are deployed overseas.

Mark Sanford, the Republican governor of South Carolina and an Air Force reservist, predicted that reenlistment rates in the Guard might suffer, given the new demands.[111] Similar concerns are being voiced about the Reserves. In October 2003 Lt. Gen. James Helmly, the chief of the Army Reserve, told the Associated Press that faltering retention was "the No. 1 thing in my worry book."[112] By January 2004, the *Denver Post* reported Reserve retention had already shown a decline, falling 7 percent short of goals. In some states, the drop-off was even more pronounced. For example, whereas the military aims for 85 percent retention in the Reserves, Colorado units were showing only a 71 percent reenlistment rate. Master Sgt. Pat Valdez, a spokesman for the 2nd Brigade of the 91st Division of the Army Reserve, concluded that many individuals "are getting out because of personal reasons, promotions at work . . . and stress on family."[113]

Those stresses are now being felt among active duty personnel. Recruitment and retention within the active duty Army had remained strong for most of 2003, but military planners witnessed a drop in the first half of 2004. Whereas the Army exceeded its reenlistment targets by 6 percent in 2003, statistics for January through March 2004 showed a 4 percent shortfall.[114]

Fearing the effects of Iraq and other post-9/11 deployments on the force, the Pentagon employed stop-loss orders to prevent military personnel from leaving the service when their terms of enlistment expired. That approach, while allowable under current law and included within the terms of each servicemember's contract with the government, has been only rarely used in the past. The first modern use of stop-loss orders occurred during the buildup for the first Gulf War in 1990, but because the war itself was of limited duration, the long-term effects of those actions were relatively limited. On the contrary, the orders issued in November 2003 applied to thousands of servicemen and servicewomen. Because the order covered the period 90 days before and 90 days after an individual is scheduled to deploy abroad, those men and women will be unable to leave the service until the spring of 2005, at the earliest. In the Army alone, an estimated 40,000 men and women had their enlistments extended against their will for some period of time in 2003.[115] According to a senior Defense Department official, as many as 19,000 troops were covered by stop-loss orders when the recruitment and retention figures were released in April 2004. Defenders of the practice assert that all persons subject to those regulations are volunteers and that the enlistment form clearly states, "My military service may be extended without my consent until six (6) months after the end of that period of war."[116] However, given that the global war on terrorism, by the president's own admission, is expected to last many years, so too might involuntary extensions. Some military officials, while calling the use of stop-loss orders a necessary evil, concede that the action "is inconsistent with the fundamental principles of voluntary service."[117]

Our men and women in uniform all know the risks and rewards of their service long before they are sent into harm's way. More than 1.4 million men and women do choose to wear the uniform every day, and an additional 1.7 million agree to do so on a "part-time" basis as members of the National Guard or Reserves.[118] But an unsustainable operational tempo poses a grave risk to our all-volunteer force. The Iraq war (and postwar occupation), combined with ongoing operations in Afghanistan and the Balkans, has placed a serious strain on our military. David Segal, director of the Center for Research on Military Organization at the University of Maryland, warned, "Our volunteer army is closer to being broken today than ever before in its 30-year history."[119]

Continued Loss of Life and the Risks of Civil War

A far more tangible measure of how the military occupation is depleting the ranks is seen in the pictures of American servicemen and servicewomen killed in Iraq. Attacks on U.S. troops and Iraqi collaborators have become a regular feature of daily life in Iraq. American forces, whether in the center of major cities or in fortified garrisons on the outskirts of population centers, will be the focal point for attacks going forward because a segment of the Iraqi population will always view such forces for what they are—foreigners occupying their homeland. Reports of violence against U.S. forces had been declining, but the events of April 2004—a month in which more Americans were killed than in any previous month of the conflict—reveal that the risks to American forces never disappeared. Every day Americans are wounded by roadside bombs, in mortar attacks, and by sniper fire. Every week a handful of those individuals do not recover from their injuries and are lost forever. Dozens more remain maimed or handicapped for life. More than 100 Americans were killed in Iraq in the first 100 days of 2004. Amidst widespread violence in dozens of cities throughout Iraq following the crackdown on Moqtada al-Sadr's Mahdi militia and the siege of Fallujah, 128 Americans were killed by hostile fire in April.[120] There is no reason to expect a change in that trend. So long as the United States maintains its military occupation of Iraq, the number of killed and wounded will increase.

Supporters of the military occupation of Iraq might characterize such sacrifices as necessary to prevent even larger attacks on Americans in the United States. But, as this report has noted, Iraq was never before a central front in the war on terrorism. To presume that the jihadis crossing into Iraq to wage holy war against the agents of the United States would be content to conduct such attacks only there, and would not also continue to plan attacks in the United States and elsewhere, is to presume that there is a fixed number of terrorists in the world whom we can eliminate. That way of thinking ignores that the American presence itself is giving rise to the creation of an entirely new group of would-be suicide bombers.

Meanwhile, attacks on Iraqi collaborators continue to rise. As the American military has fortified itself against attacks and adopted new tactics to deal with the threat of terrorism and guerrilla fighting, terrorists have shifted their attention to softer targets—civilians who cooperate with occupation forces. A handful of suicide bombers have conducted attacks in crowded assemblies or outside popular hotels. Iraqis brave enough to volunteer for police or other security-related professions appear to be a favored target.[121] Many of the attacks on Iraqi security personnel claim the lives of innocent bystanders. A coordinated attack by at least five suicide bombers outside four different policy stations in the southern city of Basra on April 21, 2004, killed 73 Iraqis, including at least 20 children.[122] Beginning in April 2004, a spate of attacks on civilian-run supply convoys claimed the lives of dozens of civilian contractors, and many more foreign nationals were kidnapped or killed by opponents of the military occupation.

Ending the U.S. occupation of Iraq and empowering Iraqis to take control of their own security—against both foreign and domestic threats—would undermine the terrorists' tortured assertions that their acts of violence are being perpetrated against Iraqis in the interest of Iraqis. Such claims would be absurd on their face in the absence of a foreign military occupation perceived to be thwarting the desires of the Iraqi people.

Sporadic acts of violence against Americans, and the equally sense-less killings of well-intentioned Iraqis attempting to take control of their country, pale in comparison to what would occur in the event of full-scale civil war. Feelings of resentment and anger will only grow as U.S. troops are seen as the primary barrier to the political aspirations of various religious and ethnic groups. If ethnic and religious hostility boils over into armed conflict, thousands of Americans will find themselves in the midst of a cauldron of hatred and unspeakable violence.

Then it gets worse. The presence of U.S. forces in Iraq, far from serving as a stabilizing influence that drives religious and ethnic hostility underground, becomes a rallying point for elevating such tensions to a fever pitch. The events of early April 2004, when U.S. military operations in and around the predominantly Sunni village of Fallujah forced thousands of Iraqis from their homes, mobilized Iraqis throughout the country. As reported by the *Washington Post*, Iraqi officials worried that American actions had "cast Fallujah as the Iraqi Alamo, a symbol of courageous resistance against over-whelming odds." Images of civilian casualties broadcast by Arabic-language news networks had driven "moderate leaders in Fallujah and elsewhere to align themselves in opposition to the coalition. Other Iraqis were inspired to take up arms."[123]

The possibility of civil war is a real problem in Iraq, but it will always be a real problem. There is a persistent danger that Iraq's disparate religious and ethnic groups cannot come to an agreement and that the country might descend into chaos. The presence of U.S. forces might inhibit certain factions from resorting to violence to settle old scores, but ill-will and resentment can linger for a very long time, meaning that American troops in Iraq would constantly be at risk.

That is an intolerable risk because a civil war, while undoubtedly tragic for the people of Iraq, would not pose a direct and imminent threat to U.S. security. Dozens of such conflicts have erupted since the end of the Cold War, but the United States has wisely remained on the sidelines. The major exception—the civil war in Kosovo between ethnic Albanians and ethnic Serbs—is notable, not as an example of how U.S. intervention can mitigate interethnic violence and pave the way for reconciliation, but rather as a mark of the futility of such efforts. More than five years after U.S. warplanes bombed Serb targets in Kosovo and the rest of Yugoslavia, attacks that resulted in as many as 2,000 civilian deaths, ethnic tensions remain high—higher, even, than before the attacks were launched.[124]

In short, it is possible—perhaps even likely—that Iraq would descend into chaos, or even civil war, following the withdrawal of U.S. troops. But that is true whether the United States remains in Iraq for 5 years or 50. Our forces may or may not be able to prevent a civil war from erupting if they stay, but it is equally clear that their very presence incites ethnic tensions and invites outside intervention. Every day that American forces remain in Iraq, they run the grave risk of being caught in the middle of a maelstrom of horrific violence.

Troops Not Needed

Time magazine's decision to honor the American Soldier as its Person of the Year in 2003 is only the latest manifestation of the rising public stature of those individuals who choose to serve. Americans are rightfully proud of our armed forces. The men and women who wear the uniform are highly motivated and exceptionally well trained. They conduct themselves with the utmost professionalism. Unlike the Iraqi army, which served solely out of fear and which fled the scene of battle the moment Saddam's regime no longer threatened their lives, our military depends on talented young men and women who willingly choose to serve their country. They do not run away when the going gets tough, but they may well walk away when their enlistments expire. The nation's ability to maintain an all-volunteer force will be impaired if our forces are spread too thin, if they are called upon to spend too many months away from their families, and if the mission being pursued is not vital to U.S. national security.

The military occupation of Iraq is not vital to U.S. security. We need not station our forces in the midst of a hostile landscape in perpetuity in order to safeguard U.S. vital security interests. That lesson was driven home during the last war. The American bases in Saudi Arabia—the same bases that had generated the resentment and anger that fed the radical Islamists' movement—were unnecessary. Hundreds of sorties were flown by aircraft launched from bases located thousands of miles away from the target area. We know of aircraft launching from the United Kingdom and tiny Diego Garcia in the Indian Ocean. Even more incredible, a number of bombing missions were conducted by aircraft flying round-trip from the United States.[125] Clearly, the American military's capacity for projecting power knows few limits. With the removal of Saddam's regime, no sensible person is contemplating another ground invasion of any country in the region. Therefore, there is no strategic rationale for retaining American forces in Iraq.

Absent strategic justifications for keeping troops in Iraq, some people point to economic or political concerns. For example, many of those who called for an end to the American military presence in Saudi Arabia, but who hoped to replace that presence with a comparable garrison in Iraq, argue that the U.S. military must remain in the region indefinitely to ensure access to the region's oil.[126] But the American military presence is not essential (and might even be detrimental) to ensuring that Persian Gulf oil reaches world markets.

Many Americans still shudder at the memories of the Arab oil embargoes of the 1970s. But despite popular perceptions, the economic effects of those embargoes were extremely limited, and it is highly unlikely that Arab OPEC governments would attempt a repeat of their failed policies of the 1970s.[127] An explicit attempt to withhold Iraqi oil from world markets might have an economic impact, but it would be a very slight one, and the effects of such a policy would certainly be more painful for the people of Iraq than for Americans. In a report published before the start of the first Gulf War, energy economist David Henderson of the Naval Postgraduate School referred to Iraq's "oil weapon" as a "dud." In the worst-case scenario, he estimated that the cost to the U.S. economy of Iraq withholding its oil would be "at most half of one percent of our gross national product, and probably much less." The average cost amounted to $112 per person, per year.[128] Those numbers were compiled nearly 14 years ago, but even if the costs were found to be twice that amount under current conditions (a purely hypothetical assumption), that would hardly constitute an economic crisis.

On a slightly broader level, others may contend that the presence of the U.S. military in Iraq is a stabilizing influence throughout the entire region. Stability in the Middle East is particularly crucial, given that military conflict can and has disrupted oil flows, with detrimental short-term economic consequences for the United States.[129] But experience shows that U.S. military forces are themselves a destabilizing influence—their mere presence is a lightning rod for dissent, and radicals use this issue to whip up anti-American and anti-Western sentiment.

Oil revenue is the key to Iraq's rebuilding effort. Iraqi oil began to flow immediately after punitive economic sanctions were lifted, and the flow will accelerate as Iraq's damaged and decrepit equipment and infrastructure are returned to operability, regardless of whether U.S. troops are stationed in Iraq. U.S. policy in the Persian Gulf should not be based on the assumption that the region's energy resources will not make it to market absent the presence of U.S. troops. It is in the interest of Iraq's government, even a government not necessarily committed to principles of Western-style democracy, to ensure that Iraq's oil reaches global markets.

A related concern is that terrorists will be able to finance their operations with Iraqi oil revenue. Indeed, bin Laden has urged his followers not to damage oil wells since oil is the source of Arab power.[130] Al Qaeda and other terrorist groups are criminal enterprises, adept at securing finances in a variety of ways, from marketing stolen consumer credit cards to drug smuggling and trafficking. That problem is not unique to Iraq, and there are a variety of ways to eliminate sources of terrorist funding. The least effective approach would be to leave the U.S. military to guard Iraqi oil fields to ensure that Al Qaeda or other terrorists don't steal a few million gallons of crude. Responsibility for ensuring that Iraqi oil revenues flow to legitimate businesses, and not terrorist coffers, must fall to the Iraqi people. In short, we need the cooperation of Middle Eastern governments to track down terrorist financing. That cooperation may be harder to come by if the United States maintains a military occupation that they loathe.

4. A Democratic Middle East Is a Chimera

The U.S. occupation of Iraq siphons resources from the fight against Al Qaeda and indirectly aids bin Laden and his ideological allies by providing them with additional excuses for attacking Americans. But what of the notions that our military presence is necessary to implant democracy in Iraq and that the spread of democracy will undermine bin Ladenism? If terrorists flourish in conditions of political powerlessness and despair, the creation of a democratic Iraq could break the cycle of terror—or so President Bush contends. In his speech at Whitehall Palace in London in November 2003, the president called for a "commitment to the global expansion of democracy, and the hope and progress it brings, as the alternative to instability and to hatred and terror." "Lasting peace is gained as justice and democracy advance," he explained, because "in democratic and successful societies, men and women do not swear allegiance to malcontents and murderers; they turn their hearts and labor to building better lives." The spread of democracy was crucial in the fight against terrorism, Bush continued, because "democratic governments do not shelter terrorist camps or attack their peaceful neighbors."[131] In his nationally televised press conference on April 13, 2004, the president reaffirmed those sentiments, declaring that there are only two alternatives: "Iraq will either be a peaceful, democratic country, or it will again be a source of violence, a haven for terror, and a threat to America and to the world."[132]

The creation of a stable, democratic, and peaceful Iraq might serve as an example for neighboring regimes and could—over time—lead to the emergence of similar democratic governments elsewhere in the Arab world. However, given the ethnic and religious cleavages that have plagued Iraq since its creation, and given the fact that Iraq lacks any substantive experience in liberal, pluralistic government, our attempt to craft such a state is likely to fail.

Democracy at Gunpoint?

It is extremely difficult, even under the best conditions, to establish democracy through military intervention. One study of regime change in the 20th century found that only 4 of the 16 operations in which the United States was involved in effecting a change in government resulted in the establishment of democracy.[133] Another analysis concluded that in only 1 of 35 cases did a "full-fledged, stable democracy . . . emerge within 10 years" after U.S. intervention. George Downs, dean of social science and professor of politics at New York University, and Bruce Bueno de Mesquita, Silver Professor of Politics at NYU, observed from their research that no country has "an enviable record of creating democracy by military intervention."[134]

Liberalization and democratization are incredibly complex and contingent historical developments—not a simple matter of imposing the right institutions by force. The growth of political freedom is closely correlated with economic growth, increasing education, the emergence of a middle class, and a sense of coherent national identity (which explains, among other things, why Germany and Japan eventually succeeded in embracing democracy following their defeat in World War II). As the Cato Institute's Patrick Basham pointed out in a recent paper, "Democracy is an evolutionary development, rather than an overnight phenomenon."[135]

Political analysts agree that, for democracy to flourish, a stable political culture has to be established in which all groups are working together peacefully, even if their individual interests are set back or compromised. Iraq is nowhere near achieving such a political culture; not only is there a lack of any substantive culture allowing open debate, dialogue, or compromise, but Iraq's incredible religious and ethnic fractiousness creates a complex, even chaotic, environment for political reform. Shia Arabs constitute as much as 60 percent of the population of Iraq. They predominate in the south but also make up large communities in central Iraq. The Shias are looking to finally leverage their numerical superiority into political power. Meanwhile, the Sunni Arabs, concentrated in the central part of Iraq, in and around Baghdad and into the north and west, aim to preserve some semblance of their long-held hegemony in the country. The Kurds defy both the Shias and the Sunni Arabs by demanding autonomy in the north. Much is at stake for those three groups, as well as for the tribes and other smaller ethnic and religious minorities (including Assyrians, Turkomen, Armenians, and even a few Jews) who constitute the Iraqi polity.

Iraq's assorted ethnic, religious, and tribal communities do not share a strong sense of national or other collective identity. The Iraqi people never really embraced the postcolonial boundaries imposed on them when the British expelled the Ottoman Turks from the region after World War I. Any concept of national identity as it exists in Iraq reflects, if anything, the respective groups' ties to outside communities—the Kurds with their compatriots in Greater Kurdistan (in Turkey, Syria, and Iran); the Shiites with their coreligionists in Iran and other parts of the Middle East; and the Arab Sunnis with the Arab nationalist movement, manifested through the Baath party, and to various other expressions of political Islam. That complex ethnic and religious cauldron explains why past governments in Baghdad that were able to maintain the territorial integrity of Iraq did so through the use of brutal military force and intimidation. The lack of common identity, combined with different perceptions of interest based on tribal, ethnic, or religious affiliation, greatly complicates the prospects for creating a representative government.

Prospects for Liberal Democracy

Given such ethnic turmoil, using American power to transform Iraq into a democracy requires the United States to juggle the conflicting demands of the various Iraqi factions and, inevitably, to choose sides. In the so-called Sunni triangle in central Iraq, the insurgent attacks continue, and the use of American power implies wrapping whole towns and villages in barbed wire, restricting the movements of civilians, and subjecting the populace to regular surveillance and occasional intrusive inspections. Events in Fallujah in April 2004, when the U.S. military responded to the ghastly mutilations of the bodies of four American contractors by launching a large-scale assault on the city, demonstrate that insurgents can draw the occupying power into bloody battles in populated areas, inflaming the local residents and increasing the cost of the occupation. American forces were forced to use war-zone weaponry such as artillery and AC-130 gunships, sometimes in heavily populated areas. The resulting collateral damage to civilian and residential property was widely reported in Arab media.

Even before the violence in and around Fallujah in April, there had been other clashes between U.S. troops and Iraqi civilians.[136] American power may also have to be applied in resolving the situation in northern Iraq, where the Kurds are attempting to reverse the ethnic cleansing practiced during Saddam Hussein's regime by forcing Arabs to leave oil-rich towns such as Kirkuk.[137] Although the Kurds have managed to convince the current Iraqi Governing Council to grant them some measure of autonomy, the Shiite majority in Iraq is unlikely to accept such an outcome and will fight to control access to the region's oil resources. Kurdish autonomy also threatens Turkey, Iran, and Syria, each of which has its own Kurdish minority. Turkey has repeatedly voiced its objections to Kurdish autonomy and may intervene militarily against the Iraqi Kurds to prevent the secession of its own Kurdish population. During a visit to Washington in January 2004, Turkish prime minister Tayyip Erdogan attempted to extract a formal pledge from President Bush that the United States would oppose Kurdish autonomy. In remarks after the Oval Office meeting, President Bush attempted to calm Turkish fears by reaffirming America's desire "for a peaceful country, a democratic Iraq that is territorially intact."[138] But if the Kurds continue to push for autonomy, or even independence, the United States will be caught in the middle.

American power would also be necessary to reconcile Shiite Grand Ayatollah Ali al-Sistani's demands for direct elections with the insistence of the Sunni clergy that such elections not be held. Still others, such as the populist Shiite cleric Moqtada al-Sadr, have long been skeptical of elections in general and have called upon their followers to oppose the U.S. occupation.[139] When Sadr rallied his militia, the Mahdi Army, to rise up against the occupation forces in April 2004, al-Sistani urged caution and a step back from violence, but his authority may wane as Iraqis tire of his moderate approach.

In the event that general elections are held, insurgent groups will likely target election officials, candidates, and even voters in an attempt to undermine the electoral process. With so much riding on the results, the use of violent tactics may spread beyond the current insurgents, and the subsequent atmosphere of fear could disrupt the elections. But even if the voting process proceeds peacefully, many of the losers will challenge the results and place much of the blame for their failure to secure a political victory on American shoulders because so long as the United States maintains its military occupation, the Iraqi government's actions will be attributed to U.S. coercion.

The impulse to challenge the legitimacy of the electoral process is not limited to a small or isolated segment of the population. Given the conflicting goals of the various Iraqi factions, there are certain to be many people who are not satisfied with the results. If the Sunni Arabs lose power to the Shiites, their recourse will be to continue the insurgency in the Sunni triangle and to expand their operations throughout Iraq in an effort to undermine the new government. If the elections are not held in accordance with al-Sistani's demands, it is likely that there will be considerable unrest among the majority Shiite population, threatening to rapidly undermine whatever minimal control the American occupation authorities have left in Iraq. On the other hand, an electoral victory by al-Sistani's associates could further radicalize rival Shiite clerics, such as al-Sadr, who have been far more outspoken in their criticism of the U.S. occupation.

Given the clear lack of most of the ingredients necessary for a successful democracy in Iraq, it would be foolish to frame the success of the U.S. mission in Iraq in terms of our ability to create a stable, pluralistic democracy there. As Middle East expert David L. Philips noted: "The tribal structures, the ethnic groupings—they matter to Iraqis. They're important. This isn't a university laboratory."[140] An aggressive strategy to install liberal democracy in Iraq will almost inevitably fail, and it could foster the very type of political situation that the United States was aiming to avert by going into Iraq in the first place: namely, the creation of a hostile, unstable, Islamist government in the heart of the Middle East.

Nascent democracy often gives birth to forms of nationalism and may also encourage ethnic and religious self-identification that challenges the authority of the transitional nation state. If the government of that interim state is supported by external powers, then those contrarian sentiments are also directed at the outside backer. That is precisely the situation that the United States faces today in Iraq, where religious and ethnic identity serve to rally individual Iraqis to a collective cause; those groups temporarily put aside their differences with one another and focus their efforts against the outsiders.

As for the possibility of creating a single, uniting state in Iraq, a federal system that would provide some autonomy for the three major communities, while establishing a central government in Baghdad, might square the circle. But such a system requires a sense of common identity that would bring the various communities into agreement on some form of a "national contract." And in any case, the concept of an Iraqi federation that subsumes competing ethnic and nationalist pressures seems highly unlikely, especially when one considers the backdrop of the disappearance of the multinational Soviet Union, the implosion of Yugoslavia, the divorce of Czechs and Slovaks, the rise of secessionist movements in Indonesia, and the survival of the French separatist movement in Quebec (not to mention the rise of secessionist and nationalist movements elsewhere—for example, Tamils in Sri Lanka, Basques in Spain, Chechens in Russia, and Kosovars in Serbia, to name just a few). Those who propose a united Iraqi state should explain why a similar national system that rejected religious and ethnic identities didn't survive in Yugoslavia but would work in Iraq. It doesn't seem that any of the communities in Iraq is ready for such an experiment. The prospects of success in the wider regional context seem no more promising, given that the only example of confederal binationalism in the Arab world, Lebanon, proved to be a total and bloody disaster.

Observations about the absence of factors supporting democratic reform, and of the risks posed to American interests by genuine democratic impulses not only in Iraq but throughout the Middle East, are affirmed by a classified State Department report released to the media a few weeks before the Iraq invasion. According to press accounts, the report prepared by the State Department's Bureau of Intelligence and Research noted that "Middle East societies are riven by political, economic and social problems that are likely to undermine stability regardless of the nature of any externally influenced or spontaneous, indigenous change." According to an intelligence official who agreed to read portions of the classified report to the *Times*, the title of the report, "Iraq, the Middle East and Change: No Dominoes," conveyed the general sentiment of the analysts who prepared it, namely that the presumption that a "democratic Iraq" will trigger a transformation of the Middle East is not based on facts on the ground.[141]

The U.S. military occupation of Iraq should not be predicated on the creation of a liberal democratic government there. A presumed need to protect and defend the nascent democracy should not be used as a pretext for extending the occupation indefinitely. Likewise, while we should be cognizant of the risks posed to brave Iraqis who cooperated with the United States, there are many ways to safeguard those individuals that do not involve the explicit protection of many thousands of American troops. In short, it is appropriate and natural that we should "hope," as Rumsfeld said in April 2003, that the Iraqis will choose "a system that will be democratic and have free speech and free press and freedom of religion," but the Bush administration should *require* only that the new government not pose a threat to the United States.[142] Rumsfeld delineated some of those conditions as well, including the removal of the Baath Party from power and a prohibition on the possession of WMD.[143] One should add to that list the requirement that the new government have no ties to Al Qaeda or other anti-American terrorist organizations.

Beyond those prudent demands on the new Iraqi government, any attempt to engineer results of Iraqi elections, or to dictate the form and function of the new Iraqi government, will only engender further hostility and suspicion. Jessica Stern, lecturer in public policy and faculty affiliate of the Belfer Center for Science and International Affairs at Harvard University, has noted that humiliation, real or perceived, is more likely to attract recruits to terror than is poverty or lack of opportunities.[144] Thus, an occupied Iraq that is forced into a semblance of a democracy is more likely to feed into global jihad concentrated on the United States than is an Iraq from which the United States exits gracefully and does not tell the Iraqis how they should govern themselves.

This much is clear: a military occupation, or even the appearance of U.S. patronage of a government that is only nominally independent, will not lead to genuine democracy in Iraq. Further, and even more important, only a government committed to cooperation in the fight against Al Qaeda and other anti-American terrorist groups can be said to be compatible with U.S. interests. The long-term object of our policy in Iraq should not be democracy per se but rather the emergence of a tolerant, liberal civil society that does not seek our destruction. Given that a tolerant liberal society is not going to emerge in the near term, we must consider the collateral effects of a lengthy military presence in Iraq during the transitional period.

5. How We Get Out

The military occupation of Iraq is counterproductive to winning the war on terrorism, enormously costly, militarily and economically unnecessary, and politically unsustainable. Meanwhile, the presence of U.S. troops does little to advance liberal democracy in Iraq and much to inhibit such political development. Notwithstanding the optimistic predictions of the Bush administration and its ideological allies, the facts are irrefutable: Iraq is many years away from becoming a stable unified democracy, and there is nothing that the United States can do to alter this state of affairs.

Already the post-Saddam "happily-ever-after" projected in the utopian prewar blueprints—the ones that said the occupation would pay for itself and that the majority of U.S. troops would be out of Iraq by December 2003—has proved to be nothing more than wishful thinking. And yet the arguments for a long-term military presence persist. Those arguments represent the triumph of hope over experience. They also ignore the dangers attendant to a long-term U.S. military occupation. Disregarding such risks, the proponents of occupation are inclined to seek more expansive ends. They are not content to define vital U.S. security interests in terms of protecting the lives and well-being of Americans. Without a clear and straightforward strategy aimed at defending vital U.S. interests, the United States is left with half measures that are unlikely to succeed and that leave American military and civilian personnel in a highly exposed and vulnerable position for an indefinite period of time.

Just before the war, President Bush defined success as a democratic Iraq rebuilt by the United States with the same kind of commitment that was shown to Germany and Japan following World War II. He repeated those sentiments in April 2004, even as the events on the ground in Iraq called into question the level of Iraqi support for the U.S. military presence. The goal of a democratic Iraq is noble and well intentioned. Certainly, in a perfect world, it is what we would want for the Iraqi people. But such an outcome is not only unnecessary in terms of core U.S. security interests; it is also unattainable in the near term at anything resembling a reasonable cost in both blood and treasure.

Those who are not prone to utopian fantasies—those who have a more realistic sense of our limited capacity for shaping Iraqi society—hope merely for a good solution: a reasonably friendly government that may or may not be democratic. Although Sen. John Kerry argued in December 2003 that "a specific timetable for self-government" in Iraq must include both "security and democracy," he seemed to backtrack somewhat in comments to reporters in April 2004.[145] "I have always said from day one that the goal here . . . is a stable Iraq, not whether or not that's a full democracy," the presumptive Democratic presidential nominee said. "I can't tell you what it's going to be, but a stable Iraq. And that stability can take several different forms."[146]

But even that might be asking for too much. As the occupation drags on, and as violence spreads from Sunni to Shiite communities and from central Iraq to regions south and west, there are no good options for the United States. Policymakers must therefore choose the approach that is least likely to bring harm to Americans, even if such an approach risks undermining American prestige in the near term.

American policymakers must begin with the recognition that Iraq's internal and external politics are subject to constant and unpredictable change and that each change creates a new set of challenges. The Bush administration should recognize that Iraq comprises three autonomous regions that have little in common. Given that the nation-state of Iraq is an artificial structure created by British imperialists, stitched together from three provinces of the Ottoman Empire, some measure of Iraqi disintegration is likely. Disintegration could take place in the aftermath of an American withdrawal, leading to the creation of what Israeli military historian Martin van Creveld predicted would become "mini-Afghanistans that will serve as havens for terrorist activities throughout the Middle East" and will attract regional players.[147] Or Washington could accept the reality on the ground today and allow for the emergence of three semi-independent republics in Iraq.

That is not to say that three semiautonomous Iraqi statelets (Kurdish, Sunni Arab, and Shia Arab) would be inevitable, although it may be the most realistic outcome. Certainly, civil war is another possibility, and the United States should not adopt policies likely to result in unnecessary violence and bloodshed. But while we feel an obligation to protect those Iraqis who risked their lives attempting to reform Iraqi society, we also recognize that U.S. security is not necessarily dependent on an Iraqi state that is devoid of all forms of ethnic and religious strife. If the United States were to establish such a standard as a precondition for U.S. security, the country would feel compelled to intervene in the dozens of other civil conflicts raging around the world today.

The Risk of Civil War

Of course, the extreme scenario of an Iraqi civil war, were such a conflict to occur, would be a tragic outcome of U.S. military intervention and would raise anew questions about the administration's original decision to wage war. But such are the risks associated with a policy of regime change. If every cloud has a silver lining, in Iraq it is that none of the three major ethnic groups is inherently predisposed to welcoming Al Qaeda into the country, so even an Iraqi civil war would not necessarily be a direct threat to U.S. security. We should adopt a liberal political asylum policy, allowing Iraqis who fear for their safety because of their association with the Coalition to come to the Unites States. Beyond that, the United States would need to keep a watchful eye on Iraq to ensure that Al Qaeda did not take advantage of a chaotic situation to establish a strong foothold there, but we should be keeping a watchful eye on all anti-American terrorists in dozens of places around the world. And we must do more than simply watch them. We must isolate them. We must eradicate them.

Al Qaeda is adept at operating in a range of security situations. The organization maintains terrorist cells in peaceful, developed countries—even in countries such as Germany where the United States maintains more than 70,000 troops. Osama bin Laden chose a base of operations in Afghanistan where the Taliban's brutal and stifling totalitarian rule was considered by some to be an acceptable alternative to open civil war. And, true to form, Al Qaeda has adapted to the situation in Iraq, capitalizing on a humiliating foreign occupation to attack the U.S.-run government and any innocent and law-abiding Iraqis who choose to cooperate with the occupation authorities.

For the United States to remain tied to the fortunes of the government of Iraq places our country, and our citizens, in a no-win situation. In stating its preference for democracy, but in opposing the democratic impulses of the Shiite majority and the Kurds' desire for autonomy, the United States already finds itself on a collision course with the wishes of millions of Iraqis. Forced to juggle various and clashing commitments, Americans, both in Iraq and abroad, could become targets for all unsatisfied Iraqis, Shiite or Sunni, Arab or Kurd. Successive American administrations, whether headed by Republicans or Democrats, would have two choices: reinforcement of a losing strategy or an ignominious exit. Given the certain political criticism that would be leveled against any government that "sold out" to terrorists in Iraq and elsewhere, it is easy to see how every month, every year, that the U.S. military remains in Iraq will make it more difficult and more costly for the United States to extract itself.

America would then face the choice of extending its military commitments in Iraq to the entire region, which would increase the potential for military confrontations with Iran, Syria, and even Turkey, or leaving the country with the Iraqi guerrillas jeering at us— a situation reminiscent of the Soviet and Israeli withdrawals from Afghanistan and Lebanon, respectively, or the U.S. withdrawal from Vietnam.

The prospects of an ignominious retreat are precisely what motivate some of the most fervent champions of a long-term U.S. presence in Iraq. AEI's Gerecht contends that America's enemies, even in the case of an "orderly withdrawal," will consider an American pullout a victory for their side.[148] Eliot Cohen of Johns Hopkins University's School of Advanced International Studies warns that "the price to be paid for" an American departure from Iraq "would be appalling."[149] To conclude that an orderly withdrawal from Iraq would not be in U.S. interests is to ignore that the Coalition Provisional Authority does not control events in Iraq, more than one year into the occupation, despite the presence of more than 130,000 troops on the ground. Implicitly, if 130,000 troops are unable to stifle a determined resistance movement, then more troops must be needed.[150] In other words, *any* withdrawal, orderly or otherwise, is unwise.

Such a proposition is untenable. According to a letter attributed to Abu Musab al-Zarqawi, a Jordanian with alleged ties to Al Qaeda, the terrorists' ability to operate in Iraq will likely diminish once the government is handed over to the Iraqis. Far from looking on an American military withdrawal as an opportunity to establish a strong base of operations, Al-Zarqawi worried about such a withdrawal and about the transition to an army and police force populated by people "connected by lineage, blood and appearance" to their fellow Iraqis.[151] The United States should therefore use withdrawal from Iraq to its own advantage, first, by reassigning resources to fight against Al Qaeda, but also by explicitly countering propaganda by the likes of al-Zarqawi, bin Laden, and other anti-American extremists who characterize the American occupation as a vehicle for asserting U.S. dominance in the region.

A smart power cuts its losses and recognizes that its security is not dependent on perfection. Our policy should be oriented toward achieving an acceptable end, one that safeguards American vital security interests at minimal cost and risk, because any attempt to "get things right" in Iraq will inevitably lead to the perpetuation of our stay in that troubled country. Getting things right means getting out of Iraq before we suffer further losses of blood and treasure and a further diminution of our political standing abroad.

By withdrawing militarily from Iraq, the United States will be broadcasting to the world—in particular the Middle Eastern and Muslim areas—that the United States has no plans to take control of Middle Eastern oil or to suppress the aspirations of the region's population. But at the same time, the United States must reaffirm its intentions and capability to protect Americans from threats, including the overthrow of governments found to be supporting anti-American terrorists.

The jihadis might try to tout a U.S. troop withdrawal as a moral victory. That message could be countered with a far more emphatic statement of our own: "We have liberated the people of Iraq from an oppressive tyrant. Now we are coming for you." But although that message might sell in the near future, it becomes less and less convincing as the U.S. occupation stretches from a year to several years. It will be a greater strategic victory for the jihadis if we stay.

And eventually we will have to leave. Americans sensibly oppose open-ended military commitments abroad; it is folly to presume that they will shoulder the burdens of an occupation of Iraq indefinitely. It is equally foolish to believe that Iraqis living under the occupation won't someday expel us from their country—on their terms, not on ours.

Given that an American withdrawal from Iraq would ultimately be necessitated by the loss of domestic public support, and given that the Iraqi people are sure to become increasingly emboldened in their demands that the occupation come to an end, American policymakers are confronted today with a clear choice. They can commit themselves to an orderly, voluntary withdrawal, now, on our terms; they can accede to a withdrawal in the future, on the jihadis' terms; or they can commit themselves, the American public, and the American military to an indefinite occupation regardless of the costs and risks. The third option serves no one's interests. Between the first two, the choice is clear. We must establish a plan for military withdrawal from Iraq. And we must adhere to that plan.

A Change of Direction

The Bush administration chose a policy of preventive war against Iraq, arguing that the risks of action outweighed the risks of inaction.[152] That policy, in effect, was based on a presumption of a swift victory and was inherently dismissive of the objections, raised prior to the war, that the removal of Hussein's regime might create conditions unfavorable to U.S. interests by destabilizing the region, fomenting ethnic conflict, and fanning the flames of Muslim resentment.

Administration officials may have reasoned that such predictions for postwar Iraq were overly pessimistic. And history may ultimately prove them right. But regardless of whether the decision to invade Iraq was right or wrong, it cannot be undone now, and the administration is responsible for crafting a strategy that minimizes the risks to U.S. security, especially the risk of terrorist attacks against the United States. Such a strategy must have as its centerpiece a clear plan for U.S. military withdrawal from Iraq. Just as the administration has set a date certain for handing over the government to the Iraqi people, it must also set a date, and establish and execute a plan, for removing all U.S. troops from Iraq.

Clearly, the major obstacle to U.S. military withdrawal is the achievement of an acceptable political outcome in post-Hussein Iraq. The argument for when, or whether, to withdraw U.S. forces is therefore conditioned on a particular understanding of what "acceptable" entails. Given the many reasons, documented above, why an expeditious military withdrawal serves U.S. interests, this report defines an acceptable political outcome in straightforward terms: the new government that emerges in post-Hussein Iraq must not support or harbor Al Qaeda terrorists or any other terrorist group that would attack the United States. Any policies not directed specifically toward those ends, and that otherwise extend the period of U.S. military occupation, are unnecessary and ultimately counterproductive.

Those specific security aims for the new government in Iraq can be achieved within a relatively short period of time and must be communicated to that government before, and after, the American military withdrawal. Indeed, we hasten to add, a U.S. military withdrawal should not signal a lack of attention to the affairs of state in Iraq. Eliot Cohen alleged that an American withdrawal would encourage the insurgents to believe that a humiliating American exit will improve the chances "that the United States would stay out of that part of the world for good."[153] It would be the height of irresponsibility for any American leader to allow that misperception to take hold. An American military withdrawal would not, and must not, signal that the United States has chosen to ignore events in Iraq any more than the American withdrawal from any other part of the world signals an inability or an unwillingness to actively defend vital American interests.

For example, we recognize that a government that is explicitly committed to policies of nonaggression toward the United States and that eschews ties to anti-American terrorists could, at some time following an American military withdrawal, be replaced by a government hostile to us. On the other hand, even if the character of the government did not change, the same people who are in place at the time of our departure could change Iraqi policy toward us from expressions of amity and cooperation to declarations of enmity and conflict. In either case, the United States would not ignore such developments. Outward expressions of hostility may merit punitive diplomatic or military measures by the United States in response, but we do not need to operate from bases within Iraq to exercise our prodigious economic and military power.

The courage to withdraw militarily from Iraq will require a sea change in White House thinking. First and foremost, it will require shattering neoconservative dreams of creating a democratic empire in the Middle East. Instead of trying to dictate outcomes and create a democracy in America's image, the Bush administration's guiding principle should be to allow the Iraqi people to create their own system of governance absent the pressure and humiliation of a foreign occupying army.

Genuine sovereignty for a new government in Iraq can be achieved only when American military personnel are removed from the country. Anything short of that will forever leave the impression that the new government does not serve the people of Iraq. A handover of political sovereignty that does not also include the removal of U.S. military personnel from the country is no more than a fig leaf. That is true even if the handover is accompanied by the superficial trappings of international legitimacy, such as membership in international organizations and recognition of new national symbols. Such a handover might be suitable for temporarily calming U.S. domestic fears of a quagmire in Iraq, but such half measures will hardly satisfy the wishes of the Iraqi people. They know that genuine sovereignty is derived from the ability to defend one's country from threats, both internal and external. They will not be satisfied with merely replacing the tyrannical autocracy of a native Iraqi with a government exercising only "partial sovereignty" and therefore perceived as serving the wishes of a foreign power.

Every day that the United States remains in Iraq in pursuit of a particular system of government, the moderates will grow weaker and the extremists will become emboldened. Instead of trying to control the various steps of the process in an attempt to engineer a perfect result, the United States should studiously avoid placing preconditions on the Iraqis that will slow progress toward self-government. American policymakers in Washington and in Iraq must direct all military and diplomatic efforts toward turning Iraq over to the Iraqi people promptly. To do so, Washington should take the following steps.

Encourage Representation for Iraq's Many Ethnic and Religious Groups

The interim Iraqi Constitution approved in March guarantees rights to religious and ethnic minorities. In the interest of calming the legitimate fears of Iraq's long-repressed religious and ethnic

communities—the Shia Arabs and the Sunni Kurds, especially—
the United States should encourage the transitional government to
include representatives from all major religious and ethnic groups,
much as the current Iraqi Governing Council already does. To the
extent possible, leaders should be chosen by the Iraqi people, not
by the U.S. Department of Defense or State, and should be granted
full authority for making decisions that move Iraq to self-government and self-sufficiency.

Do Not Insist upon a Strong Central Government Based in Baghdad

Instead of insisting on a strong central government based in Baghdad that largely mirrors that of Hussein's regime, the United States
should not object, for example, to a degree of autonomy for Kurds
in the north or Shiites in the South. That may prove to be one of
the most contentious political issues during the period of interim
government control. The Shiite Muslims on the Governing Council
temporarily postponed ratification of the interim constitution over
concerns that the document granted too much autonomy to the
Kurds. They dropped their objections in the interest of near-term
unity but have indicated an interest in revisiting the issue in negotiations over a permanent constitution. A permanent constitution must
be approved via popular referendum no later than October 15,
2005.[154]

In his press conference on March 6, 2003, before the start of the
war, President Bush spoke hopefully of a federation uniting Shias,
Sunnis, and Kurds. That may be the best solution, but the United
States should not demand it. However, if the Iraqis opt for a federal
system, the United States should, in the interest of promoting
regional stability, work with the Iraqis to reassure Iraq's neighbors
that a devolution of power away from Baghdad is not necessarily
a security threat; and, along those lines, the international community
may demand that Iraqis—including Iraqi Kurds—renounce territorial claims outside the current internationally recognized boundaries
of Iraq. If the Iraqis ultimately choose to divide the nation currently
known as Iraq into two or more states, Americans should not stand
in their way. But we must make clear that the Iraqis—or, individu-
ally, the Kurds, the Shias, and the Sunnis—will be responsible for the
defense of those states in the event of conflict with Iraq's neighbors.

Establish a Timeline for Political Transition

The United States and the interim Iraqi government should agree to a timeline for handing over full sovereignty. We propose a three-part transition plan addressing security (both internal and external), nationwide elections, and the creation and ratification of a permanent constitution. All three of those parts can and should proceed concurrently, and the deadlines for the latter two are already stipulated under the terms of the interim constitution.

Security Agreement

Immediately after the handover of political sovereignty to an interim Iraqi government, the United States and the new Iraqi government must reach an agreement establishing a timetable for the withdrawal of U.S. forces. Such an agreement, negotiated between two internationally recognized sovereign entities, will send a powerful message to the people of Iraq, and to the world, reaffirming the United States' good intentions. Equally important, such an agreement will enable the interim government to establish attainable objectives for its own self-defense. Knowing that their government will be responsible both for internal security within Iraq and for defending the country from external threats, the Iraqis will be empowered to take reasonable and sensible measures in that direction. By contrast, absent a firm pledge by the United States to relinquish security responsibilities, the Iraqis will be inclined to postpone crucial decisions about the size, character, and composition of their police and military forces.

In the course of negotiating an agreement for military withdrawal, the United States should explicitly affirm Iraq's right and responsibility to defend itself from foreign threats. Several hostile, and potentially powerful, neighbors surround Iraq. Iran is developing a nuclear weapons capability; Turkey has a large army; Syria is thought to possess chemical weapons and retains some military capabilities despite being bogged down in Lebanon; Israel possesses nuclear weapons and has demonstrated its ability to conduct military strike operations well inside Iraq. It is not unreasonable that the new government in Iraq would want to defend itself from outside threats, but that would require either the creation of a new military capable of mounting such a defense or an indefinite security guarantee on the part of the United States. We oppose the latter.

Therefore, in affirming Iraq's right of self-defense, the United States must address the concerns of neighboring countries, but in a way that does not commit the United States to employ military force to prevent a regional conflict. The most straightforward assurance that the United States could offer would be to point out that it was Saddam Hussein who initiated conflict with his neighbors on numerous occasions. Hussein used such military confrontations to excite Iraqi nationalism and simultaneously justify the repression of domestic dissent and even the elimination of his political adversaries. But the Iraqi people, weary after nearly three decades of unremitting strife and international isolation, are unlikely to wish to repeat Saddam's ill-fated military adventures. In short, Iraq's neighbors should feel no more threatened by the emergence of a stable government in the country than they did by the nation-state led by Saddam Hussein. That does not mean that Middle Eastern countries will have no security concerns, nor that Iraq will never pose a threat to them, but such is the nature of the international system. For the United States to guarantee to prevent a conflict, any conflict, from emerging in Iraq or anywhere else in the Persian Gulf region as a whole would be to commit the American people to an intolerable and unnecessary burden. Such a burden, by eroding American power, will make the United States less, not more, secure.

Election Plans

In postwar Iraq, elections will be a key test of the United States' commitment to democracy. The United States does not want to become involved in the process of certifying candidates or parties for election to public office, as has been done in Bosnia and Kosovo.[155] It would be far better if an international body, possibly the United Nations or the Organization for Security and Cooperation in Europe, certified the election results, lest the United States be blamed for thwarting the wishes of the Iraqi people by those who wind up on the losing end of the democratic process. At the same time, the leaders of the reconstruction effort must demand that international involvement in elections not become a pretext for needlessly extending the period of foreign occupation. International election monitors should be invited to participate only if they agree to the firm timeline previously agreed to by the United States and the Iraqi interim government.[156]

The parameters for such a timeline were outlined by the United Nations survey in Iraq completed in February 2004. The UN determined that nationwide elections conferring power upon a new government in Iraq could be held before the end of 2004, but the interim constitution sets a deadline of January 31, 2005, for the election of a transitional government and regional councils. A permanent government is to take office by December 31, 2005.[157] Prior to that time, an interim Iraqi administration will be empowered to govern the country. The original Bremer plan, which called for a series of regional caucuses to select the interim government, would have established a degree of separation between a new Iraqi government and the United States. The participants in the caucuses would have been carefully prescreened by the U.S. officials, but those screening processes would not have ensured that the candidates most preferred by the United States would have been chosen by caucus-goers. Ultimately, the choices would have been left up to individual Iraqis.

But Grand Ayatollah Ali al-Sistani and others objected, believing that the caucus plan would deny majority Shias the political power to which they felt themselves entitled and which had for so long been denied to them. Such sentiments are understandable, even as they are also self-serving. Nonetheless, the collapse of the caucus plan leads in only one direction: an interim Iraqi government, hand-picked by a third party—either the United Nations or the United States—will, for a period of time, possess sovereign authority over all of Iraq. Such a government will forever be tainted by its association with non-Iraqis, no matter what it does to distance itself from its creators. It is therefore in the interest of the interim Iraqi government and the government of the United States to move swiftly to full-scale, nationwide elections in accordance with the terms established by the interim constitution.

Drafting of a Permanent Constitution

It might seem incongruous for election planning to move forward concurrently with the drafting of a new constitution. Procedures for holding elections, for certifying candidates, and for determining the size and scope of the legislative authorities must be established before elections are held. However, constitutions need not specify all of the details of the conduct of elections. The U.S. Constitution does not include stipulations on the size or shape of ballots in the United States. That enduring document is similarly silent concerning procedures for qualifying candidates for office, from filing deadlines to the number of signatures required before a person's name is placed on the ballot. With the notable exception of citizenship and age requirements (e.g., Article 1, section 2 stipulates that a person must be 25 years of age to serve in the U.S. House of Representatives and that a person must have been a U.S. citizen for at least seven years), other details have typically been left up to state and local governing bodies. Indeed, the U.S. Constitution grants wide latitude to the states, and to both houses of Congress, on how to conduct their affairs (Article 1, sections 4 and 5, respectively). In short, plans for conducting elections can run in parallel with a drive to draft and ratify a permanent constitution. That is precisely what the interim Iraqi constitution stipulates, with the deadline for ratification of the permanent constitution set for October 15, 2005, and a newly elected government to be in office by the end of 2005.

The prospects for achieving an agreement on a permanent constitution improved following the Iraqi Governing Council's approval of the interim constitution in March 2004. Negotiations over the content and scope of that document were acrimonious, and at various stages the process seemed destined for failure. That the various factions represented in the Governing Council were able to put aside their differences long enough to hammer out an agreement suggests that some measure of optimism is warranted.

On the other hand, serious obstacles remain, and it is also possible that negotiators agreed to drop their most contentious demands under pressure from the United States. Individuals and groups may be choosing to bide their time and direct the full weight of their efforts to the drafting of a permanent constitution. Given that distinct possibility, it would be particularly unwise to declare at the outset that vital U.S. security interests in Iraq are contingent upon elections and constitutions. Beyond the practical consideration that we do not know what the constitution will stipulate or who or what group might be elected as the ruler of Iraq, to have our policy toward Iraq be dictated by constitutions and elections would set a dangerous, and ultimately untenable, precedent for our relations with many countries. After all, the United States maintains diplomatic ties with dozens of countries that have no written constitutions. Likewise, we have never made popular elections the sole precondition for conferring legitimacy on a government. Given the numerous ways in which an American troop presence in Iraq harms U.S. security interests, as documented in this report, our decision to remove U.S. forces should not be conditioned on the achievement of liberal democracy, complete with a written constitution, in Iraq.

Follow the Handover of Sovereignty with an Expeditious Military Exit from Iraq

The United States should follow up its military victory and the recognition of a new Iraqi government with a swift but orderly troop withdrawal from Iraq. As has been documented at length above, a permanent American military presence in Iraq is unnecessary. The surest way to turn a short-term military victory into a punishing and costly defeat would be to overstay our welcome.[158] There are many indications that our welcome has already worn thin. President Bush admitted in April that the Iraqis were "not happy they're occupied. I wouldn't be happy if I were occupied either."[159] Resentment of the occupation lingers and grows. Attacks continue on both Coalition forces and Iraqis accused of collaborating with the occupation. American policy must be directed toward ensuring that this resentment does not spread. Many Iraqi citizens will allow the Coalition forces to carry forward an interim plan for stabilizing the Iraqi government, but they will not do so if they see the process as merely legitimizing a continued military occupation. That is why the Bush administration must move beyond its vague assurances—such as the president's pledge that American forces would remain in the country "as long as is necessary, and not one day more"[160]—by publicly renouncing calls for a long-term occupation and by committing to a formal plan for withdrawal.

If we assume that the troop buildup for the Iraq war commenced in earnest in September 2002 and the war started in mid-March 2003, then it took roughly six months to deploy forces to Iraq. As of January 2004, the U.S. Army presence in Iraq numbered 130,000 troops. That number was to have been reduced to just over 100,000 by the end of May, but the rotation was temporarily halted to deal with the increased violence in early April. By late April, the Pentagon was reporting that it planned to leave nearly 140,000 troops in Iraq. Although a number of the forces currently occupying Iraq moved into the theater even after the start of combat operations, a mirror-image withdrawal would take not more than six months. For reference, in the first Gulf War the United States had upwards of 200,000 troops in theater at the high point of operations. Nearly all of those forces were withdrawn over the course of a four-month period.

The drawdown should begin immediately after the handover of sovereignty. This crucial first step will demonstrate U.S. resolve to terminate the occupation. The United States should then plan to withdraw the balance of its forces from Iraq prior to the holding of national elections, which the interim constitution stipulates must take place by January 31, 2005.

Conclusion

Leaders in the Democratic Party hope that the Iraq war and its aftermath have placed huge obstacles in George Bush's path to a second term. The prewar scenarios that the president mapped out for Americans—involving WMD, links between Saddam Hussein and Al Qaeda, and U.S. troops welcomed as liberators—haven't panned out. Further, the ever-rising costs in blood and treasure of occupying Iraq have sparked opposition to the administration's policies among the public and on Capitol Hill.

But leading Democrats have yet to offer a compelling alternative to a lengthy U.S. occupation. Few have made the case for an expeditious withdrawal, and most seem to buy into the contention that anything short of a secular, liberal-democratic, multiethnic society in Iraq will be a threat to U.S. security and therefore a failure of American policy. They seem prepared to leave American troops in the country, or even to increase the number of troops there, in order to achieve those ambitious ends. In short, given the seemingly broad bipartisan support for a semipermanent military garrison in Iraq—and given the enormous costs and risks of such a presence—U.S. policies in postwar Iraq seem headed in the direction of a bipartisan failure.

This simply continues the pattern established prior to the start of the war against Iraq. Democrats and Republicans alike bemoaned Saddam Hussein's obvious and flagrant mistreatment of religious and ethnic minorities in his country. They hoped that the presence of a democratic government in the center of the Arab world would become a shining example for the region and the world. But above all else, and particularly after the attacks of September 11, when the American public was especially sensitive to real and potential threats, our political leaders warned of the supposed threat posed by Saddam Hussein.

Although Hussein's human rights violations were never disputed and political reform in Iraq might spread beyond its borders in ways that could serve U.S. interests over the long term, we now know that the supposed threat was just that. We know that a foreign occupier is unlikely to resolve religious and ethnic tensions in Iraq and, indeed, may well exacerbate them. And although we hope for the eventual emergence of liberal democracy in Iraq, and throughout the world, we know that that will not happen any time soon.

There was bipartisan support for a war against Saddam Hussein. Republicans and Democrats alike voted to grant the president wide latitude to wage war in Iraq independent of congressional oversight. And the president wielded that authority aggressively. Now, if the president does not embrace an expeditious military withdrawal, Congress should consider forcing the issue through its control over the appropriations process.

Prior to launching the military operation that ultimately resulted in the removal of Saddam Hussein from power, the Bush administration argued that the operation would set in motion a chain of events that would ultimately democratize the entire region. That may happen, but U.S. policy should not be directed toward that end. Our overriding goals should be the protection of vital U.S. interests and the mitigation or elimination of threats to the United States. Rather than take a direct, active role in the creation of a new government in Iraq, the United States can foster an atmosphere conducive to reform there and elsewhere in the Middle East by adopting a largely hands-off approach. Such an approach implicitly concedes that the United States is prepared to accept a less-than-optimal outcome in Iraq. The United States is a superpower with noble ambitions but limited means, so it is incumbent upon policymakers to reaffirm the paramount importance of American security.

As with so many public policy issues, this means coming to grips with the problem of sunk costs. Some observers might argue that the United States has already spent so much on the Iraqi project that we must stay, that we cannot afford to leave. But for the person who finds himself in a hole, the best advice is to stop digging.

The same men and women who previously predicted that the war would pay for itself, and that postwar Iraq would quickly settle into peace and stability, will undoubtedly decry such measures as defeatism. But given that their predictions have been so dramatically off the mark, why should we listen to them?

A decision by the Bush administration to quickly hand over full political power to the new government of Iraq, and to follow on that decision by removing all U.S. military personnel from the country, will minimize the enormous costs and risks associated with a military occupation and could eventually set the stage for a stable and sustainable relationship between Iraq and the United States.

Notes

1. Niko Price, "AP, in First Nationwide Tally of Iraqi Civilian War Deaths, Counts at Least 3,240," Associated Press, June 11, 2003; and Daniel Cooney, "Morgue Records Show 5,500 Iraqis Killed," Associated Press, May 23, 2004.

2. Richard Bernstein, "Germans Free Moroccan Convicted of a 9/11 Role," *New York Times*, April 8, 2004.

3. Quoted in Eric Schmitt, "Aftereffects: The Pullout; U.S. to Withdraw All Combat Units from Saudi Arabia," *New York Times*, April 30, 2003, p. A1. See also Rowan Scarborough, "U.S. to Pull Forces from Saudi Arabia," *Washington Times*, April 30, 2003, p. A1; and Vernon Loeb, "U.S. Military Will Leave Saudi Arabia This Year," *Washington Post*, April 30, 2003, p. A1.

4. "Americans Officially End Era at PSAB," Saudi-U.S. Relations Information Service. August 30, 2003.

5. "Election 2000 Presidential Debate II with Republican Candidate Governor George W. Bush and Democratic Candidate Vice President Al Gore," October 11, 2000, C-SPAN transcript, http://www.c-span.org/campaign2000/transcript/debate_101100.asp.

6. John Kerry, "A Strategy for Iraq," *Washington Post*, April 13, 2004.

7. "Postwar Violence Threatens Stability, U.S. Resolve," editorial, *USA Today*, March 19, 2004.

8. Tom Donnelly, "There's No Place Like Iraq," *Weekly Standard*, May 5, 2003, p. 10.

9. Max Boot, "American Imperialism? No Need to Run Away from That Label," *USA Today*, May 6, 2003, p. 15A.

10. Thomas Donnelly, "Iraq Is the Central Front," American Enterprise Institute, September 24, 2003.

11. Richard Perle in "Iraq: What Lies Ahead—Black Coffee Briefings on the War in Iraq," American Enterprise Institute, April 15, 2003, http://www.aei.org/events/filter.,eventID.273/transcript.asp.

12. Donnelly, "Iraq Is the Central Front."

13. Lawrence Kaplan and Bill Kristol, "Closing In," *National Review*, February 24, 2003.

14. Reuel Marc Gerecht, "A Difficult Marriage," *Weekly Standard*, December 22, 2003.

15. Project for the New American Century, "Statement on Post-War Iraq," http://www.newamericancentury.org/iraqstatement-031903.htm.

16. White House, "President Addresses the Nation in Prime Time Press Conference," news release, April 13, 2004, http://www.whitehouse.gov/news/releases/2004/04/20040413-20.html.

17. Perle in "Iraq: What Lies Ahead."

18. Condoleezza Rice, "Transforming Iraq," Remarks at 28th Annual Convention of the National Association of Black Journalists, August 7, 2003, http://usinfo.

state.gov/xarchives/display.html?p = washfile-english&y = 2003&m = August&x = 20030808120241hsans0.2966577&t = xarchives/xarchitem.html.

19. Thomas Friedman, "You Broke It? Now You Own It America in Iraq," *International Herald Tribune*, April 10, 2003.

20. Nancy Pelosi, "Statement on Postwar Iraq," September 16, 2003, http://www.democraticleader.house.gov/press/releases.cfm?pressReleaseID = 293.

21. Edward Kennedy, "An Agenda on Foreign Policy and Defense," www.senate.gov/-kennedy/foreignpol.html.

22. Douglas Feith, "U.S. Trying to Prepare for a Post-Saddam Iraq That Will Work," Department of Defense news briefing, February 22, 2003, http://usinfo.state.gov/regional/nea/iraq/text2003/0222uspos.htm.

23. Ibid.

24. Donnelly in "Iraq: What Lies Ahead."

25. Stephen R. Weisman, "Iraq Exit Plan: New Obstacles, Some Fear Quick Shift of Power Carries Risk," *New York Times*, November 29, 2003, p. A1.

26. Fareed Zakaria, "What We Should Do Now," *Newsweek*, September 1, 2003, U.S. Edition.

27. Quoted in Dana Milbank and Mike Allen, "Bush Urges Commitment to Transform Mideast," *Washington Post*, November 7, 2003.

28. Dana Milbank and Claudia Deane, "Hussein Link to 9/11 Lingers in Many Minds," *Washington Post*, September 6, 2003.

29. White House, "President Discusses the Future of Iraq," news release. February 26, 2003, http://www.whitehouse.gov/news/releases/2003/02/20030226-11.html.

30. See, for example, Stefan Halper and Jonathan Clarke, *America Alone: The Neo-Conservatives and the Global Order* (New York: Cambridge University Press, 2003), pp. 133–35; and Ivo H. Daalder and James M. Lindsay, *America Unbound: The Bush Revolution in Foreign Policy* (Washington, DC: Brookings Institution, 2003), pp. 36–40.

31. "Geopolitical Diary," January 7, 2004, Stratfor, www.stratfor.com.

32. Quoted in John Hanna, "Myers: War Going 'Reasonably Well' But Long-Term Commitment Likely," Associated Press, April 23, 2004.

33. Josh White and Jonathan Weisman, "Limited Iraqi Sovereignty Planned," *Washington Post*, April 22, 2004. The State Department had earlier planned to have as many as 3,000 Americans stationed in the new embassy. Robin Wright, "U.S. Has Big Plans for Embassy in Iraq," *Washington Post*, January 2, 2004, p. A14.

34. J. Cofer Black, "Al-Qaida: The Threat to the United States and Its Allies," Testimony before the Subcommittee on International Terrorism of the House Committee on International Relations, April 1, 2004, wwwa.house.gov/international_relations/108/bla040104.htm.

35. "Stabilizing Iraq," *To the Point*, Public Radio International, aired June 13, 2003.

36. "U.S. Casualties in Iraq." *GlobalSecurity.org*, n.d., http://www.globalsecurity.org/military/ops/iraq_casualties.htm.

37. Josh White, "138,000 Troops to Stay in Iraq through 2005," *Washington Post*, May 5, 2004.

38. White House, "President's Remarks before the U.N. General Assembly," news release, September 12, 2002, http://www.whitehouse.gov/news/releases/2002/09/20020912-1.html.

39. White House, "President, House Leadership Agree on Iraq Resolution," news release, October 2, 2002, http://www.whitehouse.gov/news/releases/2002/10/20021002-7.html.

40. Thomas L. Friedman, "Presidents Remade by War," *New York Times*, December 7, 2003.

41. White House, "Address of the President to the Nation," news release, September 7, 2003, http://www.whitehouse.gov/news/releases/2003/09/20030907-1.html.

42. U.S. Department of State, "Patterns of Global Terrorism," Annual Report, http://www.state.gov/s/ct/rls/pgtrpt/2000/.

43. Paul Watson and Mubashir Zaidi, "Militant Flourishes in Plain Sight," *Los Angeles Times*, January 25, 2004.

44. Bush and Wolfowitz quoted in Milbank and Deane.

45. Bush quoted in Dana Milbank, "Bush Disavows Hussein–Sept. 11 Link," *Washington Post*, September 18, 2003.

46. Cheney quoted in Milbank and Deane; and Milbank.

47. James Risen, "Czech President Says No Evidence 9-11 Hijacker Met with Iraqi Spy in Prague," Middle East Info Center, October 20, 2002.

48. Milbank.

49. Rohan Gunaratna, "Iraq and Al Qaeda, No Evidence of Alliance," *International Herald Tribune*, February 19, 2003.

50. Sebastian Rotella, "Allies Find No Links between Iraq, Al Qaeda," *Los Angeles Times*, November 11, 2002.

51. Greg Miller, "Cheney Is Adamant on Iraq 'Evidence,'" *Los Angeles Times*, January 23, 2004.

52. Peter Bergen, "Armchair Provocateur: Laurie Mylroie: The Neocons' Favorite Conspiracy Theorist," *Washington Monthly*, December 2003, http://www.washingtonmonthly.com/features/2003/0312.bergen.html.

53. Richard A. Clarke, *Against All Enemies: Inside America's War on Terror* (New York: Free Press, 2004), pp. 95, 96. See also Jason Vest, "Beyond Osama: The Pentagon's Battle with Powell Heats Up," *Village Voice*, November 21–27, 2001.

54. Jason Burke, "Ghost of Al Qaeda Left Out of Story," *Guardian*, July 27, 2003, http://observer.guardian.co.uk/iraq/story/0,12239,891960,00.html.

55. Jason Burke, *Al-Qaeda: Casting a Shadow of Terror* (New York: I.B. Tauris, 2003), p. 15; and Jason Burke, "Al Qaeda," *Foreign Policy*, May–June 2004, p. 19.

56. "Iraq-Qaeda Links Doubted," *CBS News Online*, November 20, 2003, http://www.cbsnews.com/stories/2003/09/17/iraq/main573801.shtml.

57. Jonathan S. Landay and Tish Wells, "Iraqi Exiles Fed Exaggerated Tips to News Media," Knight Ridder, March 16, 2004, http://www.mercurynews.com/mld/mercurynews/news/world/8197503.htm.

58. Quoted in Jack Fairweather and Anton La Guardia, "Chalabi Stands by Faulty Intelligence That Toppled Saddam's Regime," *Telegraph* (London), February 19, 2004, http://www.telegraph.co.uk/news/main.jhtml?xml/news/2004/02/19/wirq19.xml.

59. Douglas Jehl, "U.S. Aides Report Evidence Tying Al Qaeda to Attacks," *New York Times*, February 10, 2004, p. A10; and Michael S. Doran, "Intimate Enemies," *Washington Post*, February 18, 2004, p. A19.

60. Leon Hadar, "Outsourcing the Hunt for Bin Laden," *Los Angeles Times*, April 1, 2004.

61. Tony Karon, "Al Qaeda's in the Money," *Time*, August 29, 2002, http://www.time.com/time/world/article/0,8599,345822,00.html.

62. Quoted in Glenn Kessler, "Clarke's Critique Reopens Debate on Iraq War," *Washington Post*, March 28, 2004.

63. Quoted in Greg Miller and Bob Drogin, "CIA Struggles to Spy in Iraq, Afghanistan," *Los Angeles Times*, February 20, 2004.

64. Rowan Scarborough, "U.S. Search for Bin Laden Intensifies," *Washington Times*, February 23, 2004; and Seymour Hersh, "Moving Targets," *New Yorker*, December 15, 2003.

65. White House, "State of the Union Address," news release, January 20, 2004, http://www.whitehouse.gov/news/releases/2004/01/20040120-7.html.

66. Joseph Cirincione, "The World Just Got Safer, Give Diplomacy the Credit," *Washington Post*, January 11, 2004.

67. George Jahn, "Iran Said to Renege on Nuclear Promises," Associated Press, January 20, 2004; and Henry Sokolski, "That Iranian Nuclear Headache," *National Review Online*, January 22, 2004, http://www.nationalreview.com/comment/sokolski200401220852.asp.

68. Gary Hart, "My Secret Talks with Libya, and Why They Went Nowhere," *Washington Post*, January 18, 2004.

69. Flynt Leverett, "Why Libya Gave Up on the Bomb," *Washington Post*, January 23, 2004.

70. Quoted in Jack Pritchard, "What I Saw in North Korea," *New York Times*, January 21, 2004.

71. Glenn Kessler, "N. Korea Nuclear Estimate to Rise," *Washington Post*, April 28, 2004.

72. Quoted in Kenji Hall, "U.S. Lawmaker: North Korea Says It Will Build More Nuclear Weapons," Associated Press, June 2, 2003.

73. U.S. Department of Defense, "Deputy Secretary Wolfowitz Interview with Sam Tannenhaus, Vanity Fair," transcript, May 9, 2003, http://www.defenselink.mil/transcripts/2003/tr20030509-depsecdef0223.html. See also "Wolfowitz's Comments Revive Doubts about Iraq's WMD," Associated Press, May 30, 2003.

74. Mistrust is growing even among those Iraqis who once supported the American invasion. See Teresa Watanabe, "From Allied to Alienated," *Los Angeles Times*, April 28, 2004.

75. Mark Landler and David E. Sanger, "Pakistani Chief Says It Appears Scientists Sold Nuclear Data." *New York Times*, January 24, 2004. See also "Scientist 'Sent Uranium to Libya,'" *BBC News*, February 20, 2004, http://news.bbc.co.uk/1/hi/world/asia-pacific/3505875.stm.

76. Quoted in Montasser Al-Zayyat, *The Road to Al Qaeda* (London: Pluto, 2004), p. 13.

77. Quoted in Karen DeYoung and Walter Pincus, "Despite Obstacles to War, White House Forges Ahead," *Washington Post*, March 2, 2003, p. A18.

78. U.S. Department of Defense.

79. Quoted in DeYoung and Pincus.

80. White.

81. Hanna.

82. Jeffrey Record, "Bounding the Global War on Terrorism," Strategic Studies Institute, December 2003, pp. 41, iv.

83. Walter Pincus, "Spread of Bin Laden Ideology Cited," *Washington Post*, April 4, 2004.

84. "Al Qaeda Influence Spreads," *Jane's Intelligence Digest*, December 13, 2003.

85. Tenet and Mueller quoted in Dana Priest, "Tenet Warns of Al Qaeda Threat," *Washington Post*, February 25, 2004.

86. Peter Beaumont and Anthony Barnett, "Hunt for UK Terror Cell," *Guardian* (London), January 4, 2004.

87. "Rumsfeld's War-on-Terror Memo," *USA Today*, October 22, 2003, http://www.usatoday.com/news/washington/executive/rumsfeld-memo.htm.

88. Dilip Hiro, "Bush and Bin Laden," *Nation*, October 8, 2001.

89. "Mubarak: Arabs Hate US More Than Ever," Reuters, April 20, 2004.

90. "Event Archive: King Abdullah II of Jordan," Commonwealth Club, April 16, 2004, www.commonwealthclub.org/archive/04/04-04abdullah-qa.html.

91. Quoted in "Iraq Could Become 'Terrorist Disneyland,' Experts Warn," Agence France Presse, April 8, 2004.

92. As of January 2004, as many as 12,000 detainees were being held, although Bremer indicated that many could be freed if they renounce violence and have a respected sponsor in the community. "Bremer: Iraq Detainees to Be Freed," *CNN.com*, January 7, 2004, http://www.cnn.com/2004/WORLD/meast/01/07/sprj.nirq.bremer/.

93. Karl Vick and Anthony Shadid, "Fallujah Gains Mythic Air," *Washington Post*, April 13, 2004.

94. "Poll: Iraqis Want U.S. Out of Country," Associated Press, April 29, 2004; and "Iraq Is Split on War and Its Aftermath," *USA Today*, April 29, 2004.

95. Gary Langer, "A Better Life," ABC News, March 15, 2004, http://abcnews.go.com/sections/world/GoodMorningAmerica/Iraq_anniversary_poll_040314.html.

96. Shaista Aziz, "U.S. Soldiers Trigger Happy in Iraq" *AlJazeera.net*, October 21, 2003, http://english.aljazeera.net/NR/exeres/92CA3C35-0801-4331-AA6A-D361467F4E93.htm; and Shaista Aziz, "U.S. Occupiers Compared to Mongol Looters," *AlJazeera.net*, October 15, 2003, http://english.aljazeera.net/NR/exeres/BF9658A9-C61F-474A-8651-76729523E391.htm.

97. "A Year after Iraq War: Mistrust of America in Europe Even Higher, Muslim Anger Persists," Pew Research Center for the People and the Press, March 16, 2004, http://people-press.org/reports/display.php3?ReportID=206.

98. Personnel figures from "Military Personnel on Hand by Region and Country in 12/31/2001," DefenseLink, http://www.defenselink.mil/pubs/almanac/almanac/people/serve.html.

99. Wolfowitz estimate in DeYoung and Pincus. See also Graham E. Fuller and Ian O. Lesser, "Persian Gulf Myths," *Foreign Affairs* 76, no. 3 (May–June 1997): 43; and Ravenal cited in Doug Bandow, "The U.S. Alliance with Saudi Arabia," *Cato Handbook for Congress: Policy Recommendations for the 108th Congress* (Washington, DC: Cato Institute, 2003).

100. Steven M. Kosiak, "Analysis of the FY 2004 Defense Budget Request," Center for Strategic and Budgetary Assessments, April 21, 2003, p. 2; see also Steven M. Kosiak, "Potential Cost of a War with Iraq and Its Post-War Occupation," Center for Strategic and Budgetary Assessments, February 25, 2003.

101. K. L. Vantran, "Rumsfeld Supports Supplemental Spending Request," American Forces Information Service News Articles, September 24, 2003.

102. In September 2003 the Pentagon was spending $3.9 billion per month in Iraq. Dave Monitz, "Monthly Costs of Iraq, Afghan Wars Approach That of Vietnam," *USA Today*, September 7, 2003; and Brian Knowlton, "Rumsfeld Estimates U.S. Monthly Costs in Iraq at $3.9 Billion," *International Herald Tribune*, July 9, 2003.

103. Quoted in White and Weisman, "Limited Iraqi Sovereignty Planned."

104. *Newsweek's* Fareed Zakaria noted that the United States spent more on defense ($322 billion in 2001) than the next 11 countries combined and predicted that U.S.

spending would soon "equal that of all other countries combined." Fareed Zakaria, "The Arrogant Empire," *Newsweek*, March 24, 2003, p. 26.

105. Eric Schmitt, "Senators Assail Request for Aid for Afghan and Iraq Budgets," *New York Times*, May 14, 2004.

106. "U.S. Army Adds 30,000 Soldiers in Iraq," Associated Press, March 24, 2004.

107. White.

108. Manuel Roig-Franzia, "Weekend Warriors Go Full Time," *Washington Post*, March 2, 2004.

109. Barry W. Holman, "Issues in Contracting for Lodging and Temporary Office Space at MacDill Air Force Base," General Accounting Office, GAO-04-296. January 27, 2004.

110. "Defense Policy and the Fiscal Year 2004 National Defense Budget," American Legion Message Points, http://www.legion.org/pdf/natsecurity_04.pdf.

111. Roig-Franzia, "Weekend Warriors Go Full Time."

112. Robert Burns, "Weekend Warriors Set Marks in New Era," *USA Today*, October 11, 2003.

113. *Denver Post* story excerpted in Tom Regan, "U.S. Military Stretched Too Thin?" *Christian Science Monitor*, January 9, 2004, http://www.csmonito.com/2004/0109/dailyUpdate.html?s = mets; see also Dan Fesperman, "Army Hopes It Has Enough in Reserve," *Baltimore Sun*, April 21, 2004.

114. Dave Moniz, "Fewer Soldiers Re-enlist; Army Sees Dip As War Increases Need," *USA Today*, April 16, 2004.

115. Lee Hockstader, "Army Stops Many Soldiers from Quitting," *Washington Post*, December 29, 2003.

116. James Kilmartin, letter to the editor, *Washington Post*, January 3, 2004.

117. Hockstader.

118. Christopher Langton, ed., *The Military Balance 2003–2004* (London: Oxford University Press), p. 18.

119. Segal quoted in Eric Rosenberg, "Stretched US Pilots May Quit Military," *Sydney Morning Herald*, January 10, 2004, excerpted in *Christian Science Monitor*, January 9, 2004, http://www.csmonitor.com/2004/0109/dailyUpdate.html?s = mets.

120. "2 Marines Killed in Fallujah amid Signs of Deal," *MSNBC.com*, April 30, 2004, http://www.msnbc.msn.com/id/4824213/.

121. See, for example, Paul Wiseman and Sabah al-Anbaki, "Truck Bomb outside Police Station South of Baghdad Kills Dozens," *USA Today*, February 10, 2004, http://www.usatoday.com/news/world/iraq/2004-02-10-iraq-blast_x.htm; and "Fallujah Attack Leaves 20 Dead, Mostly Iraqi Police," *CNN.com*, February 14, 2004, http://www.cnn.com/2004/WORLD/meast/02/14/sprj.irq.fallujah.attack/.

122. Pamela Constable, "Sadr's Backers Demonstrate in Basra," *Washington Post*, April 23, 2004.

123. Rajiv Chandrasekaran and Karl Vick, "Marines Say Time Running Short in Fallujah," *Washington Post*, April 23, 2004.

124. At least 28 people were killed, and hundreds were driven from their homes in fighting between Serbs and Albanians in March 2004. Daniel Williams, "In Kosovo, Two Worlds Divided by One River," *Washington Post*, March 22, 2004.

125. Loeb, "U.S. Military Will Leave Saudi Arabia This Year."

126. See, for example, Joseph McMillan, "U.S. Interests and Objectives," in *The United States and the Persian Gulf: Reshaping Security Strategy for the Post-Containment*

Era, ed. Richard D. Sokolsky (Washington, DC: National Defense University, 2003), pp. 15, 18.

127. See, for example, M. A. Adelman, *The Genie Out of the Bottle: World Oil Since 1970* (Cambridge, MA: MIT Press, 1996), pp. 109–17; and M. A. Adelman, "Coping with Supply Insecurity," in *The Economics of Petroleum Supply* (Cambridge, MA: MIT Press, 1993), pp. 510–11.

128. David Henderson, "Do We Need to Go to War for Oil?" Cato Institute Foreign Policy Briefing no. 4, October 24, 1990.

129. For further explanation of these issues, see Christopher Preble, "After Victory: Toward a New Military Posture in the Persian Gulf," Cato Institute Policy Analysis no. 477, June 10, 2003.

130. David Ignatius, "The Psyche of a Bin Laden," *Washington Post*, October 28, 2001, p. B7.

131. White House, "President Bush Discusses Iraq Policy at Whitehall Palace in London," news release, November 19, 2003, http://www.whitehouse.gov/news/releases/2003/11/20031119-1.html.

132. White House, "President Addresses the Nation in Prime Time Press Conference."

133. Minxin Pei and Sara Kasper, "Lessons from the Past: The American Record on Nation Building," Carnegie Endowment for International Peace Policy Brief no. 24, May 2003, http://www.ceip.org/files/pdf/Policybrief24.pdf.

134. George W. Downs and Bruce Bueno De Mesquita, "Gun-Barrel Democracy Has Failed Time and Time Again," *Los Angeles Times*, February 4, 2004.

135. Patrick Basham, "Can Iraq Be Democratic?" Cato Institute Policy Analysis no. 505, January 5, 2004.

136. There have been a number of incidents between U.S. troops and anti-American demonstrators in Iraq. See, for example, Larry Kaplow, "Rebuilding Iraq: Iraqis Decry Killing of Protesters," *Atlanta Journal-Constitution*, April 30, 2003, p. 6A.

137. Jeffrey Fleishman, "Iraq Melting Pot Nears Boiling Point," *Los Angeles Times*, January 26, 2004.

138. Ken Guggenheim, "Bush Tries to Reassure Turkey on Kurds," *Washington Post*, January 28, 2004.

139. Robin Wright and Anthony Shadid, "Changes in U.S. Iraq Plan Explored," *Washington Post*, January 25, 2004.

140. Quoted in George Packer, "Dreaming of Democracy," *New York Times Magazine*, March 2, 2003.

141. Greg Miller, "Democracy Domino Theory 'Not Credible,'" *Los Angeles Times*, March 14, 2003.

142. Rumsfeld quoted in Carolyn Lochhead, "Shiite Clerics Challenge U.S. Goal in Iraq," *San Francisco Chronicle*, April 24, 2003, p. A1.

143. David Westphal, "Hope amid Struggle for Democracy," *Sacramento Bee*, April 27, 2003, p. A1.

144. Jessica Stern, *Terrorism in the Name of God* (New York: Harper Collins, 2003).

145. Quoted in "Mr. Kerry Revises," editorial, *Washington Post*, April 21, 2004.

146. Quoted in Matea Gold and Peter Wallsten, "Kerry Places Stability in Iraq above a Democracy," *Los Angeles Times*, April 15, 2004.

147. Martin van Creveld, "A Lost Peace: When the Americans Leave," *International Herald Tribune*, November 19, 2003.

148. Gerecht.

149. Eliot A. Cohen, "If We Cut and Run," *Washington Post*, November 19, 2003, p. A27.

150. A recent report calls for a force of at least 200,000 international troops, including 150,000 from the United States. Center for American Progress, "Iraq: A Strategy for Progress," May 5, 2004.

151. Dexter Filkins, "U.S. Says Files Seek Qaeda Aid in Iraq Conflict," *New York Times*, February 9, 2004, p. A1.

152. See "Cheney Cites 'Risks of Inaction' with Iraq," *CNN.com*, August 27, 2002.

153. Cohen.

154. Susan Taylor Martin, "Democracy in Iraq Is a Tough Proposition," *St. Petersburg Times*, May 14, 2004.

155. See Ted Galen Carpenter, "The Balkans: International Mission Is Now a Mockery of Democratic Principles," *Los Angeles Times*, December 31, 2000; and Gary Dempsey with Roger Fontaine, *Fool's Errands: America's Recent Encounters with Nation Building* (Washington, DC: Cato Institute, 2001), pp. 95–100.

156. See, for example, Christopher Preble, "The U.N.'s Role in Post-War Iraq," Cato Daily Commentary, April 22, 2003, http://www.cato.org/dailys/04-22-03.html. For a different view, see Ted Galen Carpenter, "The U.N. Will Complicate an Iraq Exit Strategy," Cato Daily Commentary, April 18, 2003, http://www.cato.org/dailys/04-18-03.html.

157. Colum Lynch, "U.N. Plan for Iraq Foresees Elections," *Washington Post*, February 24, 2004, p. A1; and Martin.

158. See Crane and Terrill, p. vi; and Michael Eisenstadt, "Conclusion: Lessons for U.S. Policymakers," in *U.S. Policy in Post-Saddam Iraq: Lessons from the British Experience*, ed. Eisenstadt and Eric Mathewson (Washington, DC: Washington Institute for Near East Policy, 2003), p. 70.

159. White House, "President Addresses the Nation in Prime Time Press Conference."

160. Ibid.

Task Force Members

Subodh Atal is a foreign policy analyst based near Washington, DC. He specializes in geopolitics in South and Central Asia, the war on terror, and the implications of U.S. grand strategy. He has spoken on those topics on several occasions, including a presentation at the 2003 American Academy of Religion annual conference. His articles have been published in the *Mediterranean Quarterly*, the *Orange County Register*, and the Cato Institute's policy analysis and foreign policy briefing series. He also writes for the South Asia Analysis Group. He holds a B.Sc. from Delhi University and a Ph.D. from the University of Maryland.

Andrew J. Bacevich is professor of international relations at Boston University and director of the university's Center for International Relations. He is the author or editor of several books, most recently *American Empire: The Realities and Consequences of U.S. Diplomacy* (2002) and *The Imperial Tense: Prospects and Problems of American Empire* (2003). He is currently completing a book on the new American militarism.

Doug Bandow is a senior fellow at the Cato Institute and was special assistant to President Reagan. He has been published widely, including pieces in the *New York Times, Foreign Policy,* and the *National Interest.* He has also served as editor of the political magazine *Inquiry.* He has written several books, including *Human Resources and Defense Manpower* (1989) and *Tripwire: Korea and U.S. Foreign Policy in a Changed World* (1996). Bandow has appeared on a number of national television and radio shows, from *Crossfire* to *Oprah.* He holds a B.S. in economics from Florida State University and a J.D. from Stanford.

Ted Galen Carpenter is vice president for defense and foreign policy studies at the Cato Institute. He has written or edited 15 books and published more than 250 articles on international affairs. His writings have appeared in the *New York Times*, the *Washington Post*, the *Wall*

Street Journal, *USA Today*, *Foreign Affairs*, the *National Interest*, and many other publications. He has appeared on ABC, CBS, NBC, PBS, NPR, Fox News, CNN, Radio Free Europe, Voice of America, and the BBC. He holds a Ph.D. in U.S. diplomatic history from the University of Texas.

Jonathan Clarke is a research fellow in foreign policy studies at the Cato Institute. He was a career diplomat with the British Diplomatic Service; his foreign assignments included Germany, Zimbabwe, and the United States. Clarke has been published in *Foreign Policy*, the *National Interest*, *Orbis*, the *Los Angeles Times*, and the *Daily Telegraph* (London). He is coauthor (with Stefan Halper) of *America Alone: The Neo-Conservatives and the Global Order* (2004). He has appeared on CBS, CNBC, MSNBC, Fox News, C-SPAN, NPR, the BBC, and the CBC. Clarke is a graduate of Oxford University.

Michael Desch was named the first holder of the Robert M. Gates Chair in Intelligence and National Security Decision-Making at the George Bush School of Government and Public Service at Texas A&M University in 2004. Prior to that, he was professor and director of the Patterson School of Diplomacy and International Commerce at the University of Kentucky. He is the author of several books including *Civilian Control of the Military: The Changing Security Environment* (1999), and he edited *Soldiers in Cities: Military Operations on Urban Terrain* (2001). Desch has also published widely in scholarly journals and periodicals including *International Security*, the *Journal of Strategic Studies*, *Orbis*, and *World Policy Journal*. He holds a B.A. from Marquette University and a Ph.D. in political science from the University of Chicago.

Leon T. Hadar is a research fellow in foreign policy studies at the Cato Institute, specializing in foreign policy, international trade, the Middle East, and Asia. He is the former United Nations bureau chief for the *Jerusalem Post* and is currently the Washington correspondent for the *Singapore Business Times*. His writings have appeared in the *New York Times*, the *Washington Post*, the *Christian Science Monitor*, *Foreign Affairs*, *Current History*, and *Mediterranean Quarterly*. Hadar holds degrees from Hebrew University in Jerusalem and Columbia University. His Ph.D. in international relations is from American University.

82

Charles V. Peña is the Cato Institute's director of defense policy studies. He is the author of several studies on missile defense, arms control, space policy, and terrorism. His work has appeared in a wide variety of publications, including the *New York Times*, the *Financial Times*, the *Congressional Quarterly*, and *Wired*. Peña is a regular contributor to MSNBC and has also appeared on CNN, Fox News, NPR, Radio Free Europe, Voice of America, Univision, and BBC world television and radio. He is a graduate of Claremont Men's College and has an M.A. in security policy studies from George Washington University.

Christopher A. Preble is director of foreign policy studies at the Cato Institute. His work has been published in *USA Today, Reason*, the *Washington Times, Political Science Quarterly*, and the *Journal of Military History*, among other publications. Preble has appeared on CNN, MSNBC, CNBC, Fox News, NPR, Voice of America, CTV News (Canada), and BBC television and radio. He is the author of the forthcoming book *John F. Kennedy and the Missile Gap*. Preble was a commissioned officer in the U.S. Navy and is a veteran of the first Gulf War. He holds a B.A. from George Washington University and a Ph.D. in history from Temple University.

William Ruger is a fellow at Liberty Fund, Inc. Before joining Liberty Fund, he taught international relations at Wesleyan University and Brigham Young University. Ruger's writing has appeared in a number of publications including, most recently, *Reason, First Things*, and *Armed Forces and Society*. Ruger is also a Cato Institute research fellow in foreign policy studies and an expert on international relations, U.S. foreign policy, and civil-military relations. He earned his Ph.D. in politics from Brandeis University and holds an A.B. from the College of William and Mary.

Cato Institute

Founded in 1977, the Cato Institute is a public policy research foundation dedicated to broadening the parameters of policy debate to allow consideration of more options that are consistent with the traditional American principles of limited government, individual liberty, and peace. To that end, the Institute strives to achieve greater involvement of the intelligent, concerned lay public in questions of policy and the proper role of government.

The Institute is named for *Cato's Letters*, libertarian pamphlets that were widely read in the American Colonies in the early 18th century and played a major role in laying the philosophical foundation for the American Revolution.

Despite the achievement of the nation's Founders, today virtually no aspect of life is free from government encroachment. A pervasive intolerance for individual rights is shown by government's arbitrary intrusions into private economic transactions and its disregard for civil liberties.

To counter that trend, the Cato Institute undertakes an extensive publications program that addresses the complete spectrum of policy issues. Books, monographs, and shorter studies are commissioned to examine the federal budget, Social Security, regulation, military spending, international trade, and myriad other issues. Major policy conferences are held throughout the year, from which papers are published thrice yearly in the *Cato Journal*. The Institute also publishes the quarterly magazine *Regulation*.

In order to maintain its independence, the Cato Institute accepts no government funding. Contributions are received from foundations, corporations, and individuals, and other revenue is generated from the sale of publications. The Institute is a nonprofit, tax-exempt, educational foundation under Section 501(c)3 of the Internal Revenue Code.

CATO INSTITUTE
1000 Massachusetts Ave., N.W.
Washington, D.C. 20001
www.cato.org